THE

C

PROGRAMMING

LANGUAGE

THE

C

PROGRAMMING

LANGUAGE

Brian W. Kernighan

Dennis M. Ritchie

Bell Laboratories
Murray Hill, New Jersey

PRENTICE-HALL, INC., Englewood Cliffs, New Jersey 07632

Library of Congress Cataloging in Publication Data

KERNIGHAN, BRIAN W.
    The C programming language.

    Includes index.
    1. C (Computer program language)   I. RITCHIE,
DENNIS M., joint author.   II. Title.
QA76.73.C15K47   001.6′424   77-28983
ISBN 0-13-110163-3

The Publisher offers discounts on this book when ordered in bulk quantities. For more information write:

Special Sales/College Marketing
Prentice-Hall, Inc.
College Technical and Reference Division
Englewood Cliffs, N.J.   07632

This book was set in Times Roman and Courier 12 by the authors, using a Graphic Systems phototypesetter driven by a PDP-11/70 running under the UNIX operating system.

UNIX is a Trademark of Bell Laboratories.

25 24 23 22

PRENTICE-HALL INTERNATIONAL, INC., London
PRENTICE-HALL OF AUSTRALIA PTY. LIMITED, Sydney
PRENTICE-HALL OF CANADA, LTD., Toronto
PRENTICE-HALL OF INDIA PRIVATE LIMITED, New Delhi
PRENTICE-HALL OF JAPAN, INC., Tokyo
PRENTICE-HALL OF SOUTHEAST ASIA PTE. LTD., Singapore
WHITEHALL BOOKS LIMITED, Wellington, New Zealand

CONTENTS

PREFACE

C is a general-purpose programming language which features economy of expression, modern control flow and data structures, and a rich set of operators. C is not a "very high level" language, nor a "big" one, and is not specialized to any particular area of application. But its absence of restrictions and its generality make it more convenient and effective for many tasks than supposedly more powerful languages.

C was originally designed for and implemented on the UNIX† operating system on the DEC PDP-11, by Dennis Ritchie. The operating system, the C compiler, and essentially all UNIX applications programs (including all of the software used to prepare this book) are written in C. Production compilers also exist for several other machines, including the IBM System/370, the Honeywell 6000, and the Interdata 8/32. C is not tied to any particular hardware or system, however, and it is easy to write programs that will run without change on any machine that supports C.

This book is meant to help the reader learn how to program in C. It contains a tutorial introduction to get new users started as soon as possible, separate chapters on each major feature, and a reference manual. Most of the treatment is based on reading, writing and revising examples, rather than on mere statements of rules. For the most part, the examples are complete, real programs, rather than isolated fragments. All examples have been tested directly from the text, which is in machine-readable form. Besides showing how to make effective use of the language, we have also tried where possible to illustrate useful algorithms and principles of good style and sound design.

The book is not an introductory programming manual; it assumes some familiarity with basic programming concepts like variables, assignment statements, loops, and functions. Nonetheless, a novice programmer should be able to read along and pick up the language, although access to a more

---

† UNIX is a Trademark of Bell Laboratories. The UNIX operating system is available under license from Western Electric, Greensboro, N. C.

knowledgeable colleague will help.

In our experience, C has proven to be a pleasant, expressive, and versatile language for a wide variety of programs. It is easy to learn, and it wears well as one's experience with it grows. We hope that this book will help you to use it well.

The thoughtful criticisms and suggestions of many friends and colleagues have added greatly to this book and to our pleasure in writing it. In particular, Mike Bianchi, Jim Blue, Stu Feldman, Doug McIlroy, Bill Roome, Bob Rosin, and Larry Rosler all read multiple versions with care. We are also indebted to Al Aho, Steve Bourne, Dan Dvorak, Chuck Haley, Debbie Haley, Marion Harris, Rick Holt, Steve Johnson, John Mashey, Bob Mitze, Ralph Muha, Peter Nelson, Elliot Pinson, Bill Plauger, Jerry Spivack, Ken Thompson, and Peter Weinberger for helpful comments at various stages, and to Mike Lesk and Joe Ossanna for invaluable assistance with typesetting.

Brian W. Kernighan

Dennis M. Ritchie

CHAPTER 0: **INTRODUCTION**

C is a general-purpose programming language. It has been closely associated with the UNIX system, since it was developed on that system, and
since UNIX and its software are written in C. The language, however, is not
tied to any one operating system or machine; and although it has been called
a "system programming language" because it is useful for writing operating
systems, it has been used equally well to write major numerical, text-
processing, and data-base programs.

C is a relatively "low level" language. This characterization is not
pejorative; it simply means that C deals with the same sort of objects that
most computers do, namely characters, numbers, and addresses. These may
be combined and moved about with the usual arithmetic and logical operators implemented by actual machines.

C provides no operations to deal directly with composite objects such as
character strings, sets, lists, or arrays considered as a whole. There is no
analog, for example, of the PL/I operations which manipulate an entire
array or string. The language does not define any storage allocation facility
other than static definition and the stack discipline provided by the local
variables of functions: there is no heap or garbage collection like that provided by Algol 68. Finally, C itself provides no input-output facilities: there
are no READ or WRITE statements, and no wired-in file access methods.
All of these higher-level mechanisms must be provided by explicitly-called
functions.

Similarly, C offers only straightforward, single-thread control flow constructions: tests, loops, grouping, and subprograms, but not multiprogram-
ming, parallel operations, synchronization, or coroutines.

Although the absence of some of these features may seem like a grave
deficiency ("You mean I have to call a function to compare two character
strings?"), keeping the language down to modest dimensions has brought
real benefits. Since C is relatively small, it can be described in a small
space, and learned quickly. A compiler for C can be simple and compact.
Compilers are also easily written; using current technology, one can expect
to prepare a compiler for a new machine in a couple of months, and to find

that 80 percent of the code of a new compiler is common with existing ones. This provides a high degree of language mobility. Because the data types and control structures provided by C are supported directly by most existing computers, the run-time library required to implement self-contained programs is tiny. On the PDP-11, for example, it contains only the routines to do 32-bit multiplication and division and to perform the subroutine entry and exit sequences. Of course, each implementation provides a comprehensive, compatible library of functions to carry out I/O, string handling, and storage allocation operations, but since they are called only explicitly, they can be avoided if required; they can also be written portably in C itself.

Again because the language reflects the capabilities of current computers, C programs tend to be efficient enough that there is no compulsion to write assembly language instead. The most obvious example of this is the UNIX operating system itself, which is written almost entirely in C. Of 13000 lines of system code, only about 800 lines at the very lowest level are in assembler. In addition, essentially all of UNIX applications software is written in C; the vast majority of UNIX users (including one of the authors of this book) do not even know the PDP-11 assembly language.

Although C matches the capabilities of many computers, it is independent of any particular machine architecture, and so with a little care it is easy to write "portable" programs, that is, programs which can be run without change on a variety of hardware. It is now routine in our environment that software developed on UNIX is transported to the local Honeywell, IBM and Interdata systems. In fact, the C compilers and run-time support on these four machines are much more compatible than the supposedly ANSI standard versions of Fortran. The UNIX operating system itself now runs on both the PDP-11 and the Interdata 8/32. Outside of programs which are necessarily somewhat machine-dependent like the compiler, assembler, and debugger, the software written in C is identical on both machines. Within the operating system itself, the 7000 lines of code outside of the assembly language support and the I/O device handlers is about 95 percent identical.

For programmers familiar with other languages, it may prove helpful to mention a few historical, technical, and philosophical aspects of C, for contrast and comparison.

Many of the most important ideas of C stem from the considerably older, but still quite vital, language BCPL, developed by Martin Richards. The influence of BCPL on C proceeded indirectly through the language B, which was written by Ken Thompson in 1970 for the first UNIX system on the PDP-7.

Although it shares several characteristic features with BCPL, C is in no sense a dialect of it. BCPL and B are "typeless" languages: the only data type is the machine word, and access to other kinds of objects is by special operators or function calls. In C, the fundamental data objects are charac-ters, integers of several sizes, and floating point numbers. In addition, there is a hierarchy of derived data types created with pointers, arrays, structures, unions, and functions.

C provides the fundamental flow-control constructions required for well-structured programs: statement grouping; decision making (if); loop-ing with the termination test at the top (while, for), or at the bottom (do); and selecting one of a set of possible cases (switch). (All of these were provided in BCPL as well, though with somewhat different syntax; that language anticipated the vogue for "structured programming" by several years.)

C provides pointers and the ability to do address arithmetic. The argu-ments to functions are passed by copying the value of the argument, and it is impossible for the called function to change the actual argument in the caller. When it is desired to achieve "call by reference," a pointer may be passed explicitly, and the function may change the object to which the pointer points. Array names are passed as the location of the array origin, so array arguments are effectively call by reference.

Any function may be called recursively, and its local variables are typi-cally "automatic," or created anew with each invocation. Function definitions may not be nested but variables may be declared in a block-structured fashion. The functions of a C program may be compiled separately. Variables may be internal to a function, external but known only within a single source file, or completely global. Internal variables may be automatic or static. Automatic variables may be placed in registers for increased efficiency, but the register declaration is only a hint to the com-piler, and does not refer to specific machine registers.

C is not a strongly-typed language in the sense of Pascal or Algol 68. It is relatively permissive about data conversion, although it will not automati-cally convert data types with the wild abandon of PL/I. Existing compilers provide no run-time checking of array subscripts, argument types, etc.

For those situations where strong type checking is desirable, a separate version of the compiler is used. This program is called *lint*, apparently because it picks bits of fluff from one's programs. *lint* does not generate code, but instead applies a very strict check to as many aspects of a program as can be verified at compile and load time. It detects type mismatches, inconsistent argument usage, unused or apparently uninitialized variables, potential portability difficulties, and the like. Programs which pass unscathed through *lint* enjoy, with few exceptions, freedom from type errors about as complete as do, for example, Algol 68 programs. We will mention other *lint* capabilities as the occasion arises.

Finally, C, like any other language, has its blemishes. Some of the operators have the wrong precedence; some parts of the syntax could be better; there are several versions of the language extant, differing in minor ways. Nonetheless, C has proven to be an extremely effective and expressive language for a wide variety of programming applications.

The rest of the book is organized as follows. Chapter 1 is a tutorial introduction to the central part of C. The purpose is to get the reader started as quickly as possible, since we believe strongly that the only way to learn a new language is to write programs in it. The tutorial does assume a working knowledge of the basic elements of programming; there is no explanation of computers, of compilation, nor of the meaning of an expression like n=n+1. Although we have tried where possible to show useful programming techniques, the book is not intended to be a reference work on data structures and algorithms; when forced to a choice, we have concentrated on the language.

Chapters 2 through 6 discuss various aspects of C in more detail, and rather more formally, than does Chapter 1, although the emphasis is still on examples of complete, useful programs, rather than isolated fragments. Chapter 2 deals with the basic data types, operators and expressions. Chapter 3 treats control flow: if-else, while, for, etc. Chapter 4 covers functions and program structure — external variables, scope rules, and so on. Chapter 5 discusses pointers and address arithmetic. Chapter 6 contains the details of structures and unions.

Chapter 7 describes the standard C I/O library, which provides a common interface to the operating system. This I/O library is supported on all machines that support C, so programs which use it for input, output, and other system functions can be moved from one system to another essentially without change.

Chapter 8 describes the interface between C programs and the UNIX operating system, concentrating on input/output, the file system, and portability. Although some of this chapter is UNIX-specific, programmers who are not using a UNIX system should still find useful material here, including some insight into how one version of the standard library is implemented, and suggestions on achieving portable code.

Appendix A contains the C reference manual. This is the "official" statement of the syntax and semantics of C, and (except for one's own compiler) the final arbiter of any ambiguities and omissions from the earlier chapters.

Since C is an evolving language that exists on a variety of systems, some of the material in this book may not correspond to the current state of development for a particular system. We have tried to steer clear of such problems, and to warn of potential difficulties. When in doubt, however, we have generally chosen to describe the PDP-11 UNIX situation, since that is the environment of the majority of C programmers. Appendix A also describes implementation differences on the major C systems.

CHAPTER 1: **A TUTORIAL INTRODUCTION**

Let us begin with a quick introduction to C. Our aim is to show the essential elements of the language in real programs, but without getting bogged down in details, formal rules, and exceptions. At this point, we are not trying to be complete or even precise (save that the examples are meant to be correct). We want to get you as quickly as possible to the point where you can write useful programs, and to do that we have to concentrate on the basics: variables and constants, arithmetic, control flow, functions, and the rudiments of input and output. We are quite intentionally leaving out of this chapter features of C which are of vital importance for writing bigger programs. These include pointers, structures, most of C's rich set of operators, several control flow statements, and myriad details.

This approach has its drawbacks, of course. Most notable is that the complete story on any particular language feature is not found in a single place, and the tutorial, by being brief, may also mislead. And because they can not use the full power of C, the examples are not as concise and elegant as they might be. We have tried to minimize these effects, but be warned.

Another drawback is that later chapters will necessarily repeat some of this chapter. We hope that the repetition will help you more than it annoys.

In any case, experienced programmers should be able to extrapolate from the material in this chapter to their own programming needs. Beginners should supplement it by writing small, similar programs of their own. Both groups can use it as a framework on which to hang the more detailed descriptions that begin in Chapter 2.

1.1 Getting Started

The only way to learn a new programming language is by writing programs in it. The first program to write is the same for all languages:

Print the words
```
        hello, world
```

This is the basic hurdle; to leap over it you have to be able to create the

5

program text somewhere, compile it successfully, load it, run it, and find out where your output went. With these mechanical details mastered, everything else is comparatively easy.

In C, the program to print "hello, world" is

```
main()
{
        printf("hello, world\n");
}
```

Just how to run this program depends on the system you are using. As a specific example, on the UNIX operating system you must create the source program in a file whose name ends in ".c", such as *hello.c*, then compile it with the command

> *cc hello.c*

If you haven't botched anything, such as omitting a character or misspelling something, the compilation will proceed silently, and make an executable file called *a.out*. Running that by the command

> *a.out*

will produce

```
hello, world
```

as its output. On other systems, the rules will be different; check with a local expert.

Exercise 1-1. Run this program on your system. Experiment with leaving out parts of the program, to see what error messages you get. □

Now for some explanations about the program itself. A C program, whatever its size, consists of one or more "functions" which specify the actual computing operations that are to be done. C functions are similar to the functions and subroutines of a Fortran program or the procedures of PL/I, Pascal, etc. In our example, main is such a function. Normally you are at liberty to give functions whatever names you like, but main is a special name — your program begins executing at the beginning of main. This means that every program *must* have a main somewhere. main will usually invoke other functions to perform its job, some coming from the same program, and others from libraries of previously written functions.

One method of communicating data between functions is by arguments. The parentheses following the function name surround the argument list; here main is a function of no arguments, indicated by (). The braces { } enclose the statements that make up the function; they are analogous to the DO-END of PL/I, or the begin-end of Algol, Pascal, and so on. A function is invoked by naming it, followed by a parenthesized list of arguments.

There is no CALL statement as there is in Fortran or PL/I. The parentheses must be present even if there are no arguments.

The line that says

```
printf("hello, world\n");
```

is a function call, which calls a function named `printf`, with the argument `"hello, world\n"`. `printf` is a library function which prints output on the terminal (unless some other destination is specified). In this case it prints the string of characters that make up its argument.

A sequence of any number of characters enclosed in the double quotes `"..."` is called a *character string* or *string constant*. For the moment our only use of character strings will be as arguments for `printf` and other functions.

The sequence \n in the string is C notation for the *newline character*, which when printed advances the terminal to the left margin on the next line. If you leave out the \n (a worthwhile experiment), you will find that your output is not terminated by a line feed. The only way to get a newline character into the `printf` argument is with \n; if you try something like

```
printf("hello, world
");
```

the C compiler will print unfriendly diagnostics about missing quotes.

`printf` never supplies a newline automatically, so multiple calls may be used to build up an output line in stages. Our first program could just as well have been written

```
main()
{
    printf("hello, ");
    printf("world");
    printf("\n");
}
```

to produce an identical output.

Notice that \n represents only a single character. An *escape sequence* like \n provides a general and extensible mechanism for representing hard-to-get or invisible characters. Among the others that C provides are \t for tab, \b for backspace, \" for the double quote, and \\ for the backslash itself.

Exercise 1-2. Experiment to find out what happens when `printf`'s argument string contains \x, where **x** is some character not listed above. □

1.2   Variables and Arithmetic

The next program prints the following table of Fahrenheit temperatures and their centigrade or Celsius equivalents, using the formula $C = (5/9)(F-32)$.

```
  0   -17.8
 20    -6.7
 40     4.4
 60    15.6
...     ...
260   126.7
280   137.8
300   148.9
```

Here is the program itself.

```c
/* print Fahrenheit-Celsius table
     for f = 0, 20, ..., 300 */
main()
{
    int lower, upper, step;
    float fahr, celsius;

    lower = 0;      /* lower limit of temperature table */
    upper = 300;    /* upper limit */
    step = 20;      /* step size */

    fahr = lower;
    while (fahr <= upper) {
        celsius = (5.0/9.0) * (fahr-32.0);
        printf("%4.0f %6.1f\n", fahr, celsius);
        fahr = fahr + step;
    }
}
```

The first two lines

```c
/* print Fahrenheit-Celsius table
     for f = 0, 20, ..., 300 */
```

are a *comment*, which in this case explains briefly what the program does. Any characters between /* and */ are ignored by the compiler; they may be used freely to make a program easier to understand. Comments may appear anywhere a blank or newline can.

In C, *all* variables must be declared before use, usually at the beginning of the function before any executable statements. If you forget a declaration, you will get a diagnostic from the compiler. A declaration consists of a *type* and a list of variables which have that type, as in

```
int lower, upper, step;
float fahr, celsius;
```

The type `int` implies that the variables listed are *integers*; `float` stands for *floating point*, i.e., numbers which may have a fractional part. The precision of both `int` and `float` depends on the particular machine you are using. On the PDP-11, for instance, an `int` is a 16-bit signed number, that is, one which lies between -32768 and $+32767$. A `float` number is a 32-bit quantity, which amounts to about seven significant digits, with magnitude between about 10^{-38} and 10^{+38}. Chapter 2 lists sizes for other machines.

C provides several other basic data types besides `int` and `float`:

`char`	character — a single byte
`short`	short integer
`long`	long integer
`double`	double-precision floating point

The sizes of these objects are also machine-dependent; details are in Chapter 2. There are also *arrays*, *structures* and *unions* of these basic types, *pointers* to them, and *functions* that return them, all of which we will meet in due course.

Actual computation in the temperature conversion program begins with the assignments

```
lower = 0;
upper = 300;
step = 20;
fahr = lower;
```

which set the variables to their starting values. Individual statements are terminated by semicolons.

Each line of the table is computed the same way, so we use a loop which repeats once per line; this is the purpose of the `while` statement

```
while (fahr <= upper) {
    ...
}
```

The condition in parentheses is tested. If it is true (`fahr` is less than or equal to `upper`), the body of the loop (all of the statements enclosed by the braces { and }) is executed. Then the condition is re-tested, and if true, the body is executed again. When the test becomes false (`fahr` exceeds `upper`) the loop ends, and execution continues at the statement that follows the loop. There are no further statements in this program, so it terminates.

The body of a `while` can be one or more statements enclosed in braces, as in the temperature converter, or a single statement without braces, as in

```
while (i < j)
    i = 2 * i;
```

In either case, the statements controlled by the `while` are indented by one tab stop so you can see at a glance what statements are inside the loop. The indentation emphasizes the logical structure of the program. Although C is quite permissive about statement positioning, proper indentation and use of white space are critical in making programs easy for people to read. We recommend writing only one statement per line, and (usually) leaving blanks around operators. The position of braces is less important; we have chosen one of several popular styles. Pick a style that suits you, then use it consistently.

Most of the work gets done in the body of the loop. The Celsius temperature is computed and assigned to `celsius` by the statement

```
celsius = (5.0/9.0) * (fahr-32.0);
```

The reason for using 5.0/9.0 instead of the simpler looking 5/9 is that in C, as in many other languages, integer division *truncates,* so any fractional part is discarded. Thus 5/9 is zero and of course so would be all the temperatures. A decimal point in a constant indicates that it is floating point, so 5.0/9.0 is 0.555..., which is what we want.

We also wrote 32.0 instead of 32, even though since `fahr` is a `float`, 32 would be automatically converted to `float` (to 32.0) before the subtraction. As a matter of style, it's wise to write floating point constants with explicit decimal points even when they have integral values; it emphasizes their floating point nature for human readers, and ensures that the compiler will see things your way too.

The detailed rules for when integers are converted to floating point are in Chapter 2. For now, notice that the assignment

```
fahr = lower;
```

and the test

```
while (fahr <= upper)
```

both work as expected — the `int` is converted to `float` before the operation is done.

This example also shows a bit more of how `printf` works. `printf` is actually a general-purpose format conversion function, which we will describe completely in Chapter 7. Its first argument is a string of characters to be printed, with each `%` sign indicating where one of the other (second, third, ...) arguments is to be substituted, and what form it is to be printed in. For instance, in the statement

```
printf("%4.0f %6.1f\n", fahr, celsius);
```

the conversion specification `%4.0f` says that a floating point number is to be printed in a space at least four characters wide, with no digits after the decimal point. `%6.1f` describes another number to occupy at least six spaces, with 1 digit after the decimal point, analogous to the `F6.1` of Fortran or the `F(6,1)` of PL/I. Parts of a specification may be omitted: `%6f` says that the number is to be at least six characters wide; `%.2f` requests two places after the decimal point, but the width is not constrained; and `%f` merely says to print the number as floating point. `printf` also recognizes `%d` for decimal integer, `%o` for octal, `%x` for hexadecimal, `%c` for character, `%s` for character string, and `%%` for `%` itself.

Each `%` construction in the first argument of `printf` is paired with its corresponding second, third, etc., argument; they must line up properly by number and type, or you'll get meaningless answers.

By the way, `printf` is *not* part of the C language; there is no input or output defined in C itself. There is nothing magic about `printf`; it is just a useful function which is part of the standard library of routines that are normally accessible to C programs. In order to concentrate on C itself, we won't talk much about I/O until Chapter 7. In particular, we will defer formatted input until then. If you have to input numbers, read the discussion of the function `scanf` in Chapter 7, section 7.4. `scanf` is much like `printf`, except that it reads input instead of writing output.

Exercise 1-3. Modify the temperature conversion program to print a heading above the table. □

Exercise 1-4. Write a program to print the corresponding Celsius to Fahrenheit table. □

1.3 The For Statement

As you might expect, there are plenty of different ways to write a program; let's try a variation on the temperature converter.

```
main()     /* Fahrenheit-Celsius table */
{
    int fahr;

    for (fahr = 0; fahr <= 300; fahr = fahr + 20)
        printf("%4d %6.1f\n", fahr, (5.0/9.0)*(fahr-32));
}
```

This produces the same answers, but it certainly looks different. One major change is the elimination of most of the variables; only `fahr` remains, as an `int` (to show the `%d` conversion in `printf`). The lower and upper limits and the step size appear only as constants in the `for` statement, itself a new construction, and the expression that computes the Celsius temperature now appears as the third argument of `printf` instead of in a separate assignment statement.

This last change is an instance of a quite general rule in C — in any context where it is permissible to use the value of a variable of some type, you can use an expression of that type. Since the third argument of `printf` has to be a floating point value to match the `%6.1f`, any floating point expression can occur there.

The `for` itself is a loop, a generalization of the `while`. If you compare it to the earlier `while`, its operation should be clear. It contains three parts, separated by semicolons. The first part

```
fahr = 0
```

is done once, before the loop proper is entered. The second part is the test or condition that controls the loop:

```
fahr <= 300
```

This condition is evaluated; if it is true, the body of the loop (here a single `printf`) is executed. Then the re-initialization step

```
fahr = fahr + 20
```

is done, and the condition re-evaluated. The loop terminates when the condition becomes false. As with the `while`, the body of the loop can be a single statement, or a group of statements enclosed in braces. The initialization and re-initialization parts can be any single expression.

The choice between `while` and `for` is arbitrary, based on what seems clearer. The `for` is usually appropriate for loops in which the initialization and re-initialization are single statements and logically related, since it is more compact than `while` and keeps the loop control statements together in one place.

Exercise 1-5. Modify the temperature conversion program to print the table in reverse order, that is, from 300 degrees to 0. □

1.4   Symbolic Constants

A final observation before we leave temperature conversion forever. It's bad practice to bury "magic numbers" like 300 and 20 in a program; they convey little information to someone who might have to read the program later, and they are hard to change in a systematic way. Fortunately, C provides a way to avoid such magic numbers. With the `#define` construction, at the beginning of a program you can define a *symbolic name* or *symbolic constant* to be a particular string of characters. Thereafter, the compiler will replace all unquoted occurrences of the name by the corresponding

string. The replacement for the name can actually be any text at all; it is
not limited to numbers.

```
#define    LOWER    0         /* lower limit of table */
#define    UPPER    300       /* upper limit */
#define    STEP     20        /* step size */

main()     /* Fahrenheit-Celsius table */
{
        int fahr;

        for (fahr = LOWER; fahr <= UPPER; fahr = fahr + STEP)
            printf("%4d %6.1f\n", fahr, (5.0/9.0)*(fahr-32));
}
```

The quantities LOWER, UPPER and STEP are constants, so they do not
appear in declarations. Symbolic names are commonly written in upper case
so they can be readily distinguished from lower case variable names. Notice
that there is no semicolon at the end of a definition. Since the whole line
after the defined name is substituted, there would be too many semicolons
in the for.

1.5   A Collection of Useful Programs

We are now going to consider a family of related programs for doing
simple operations on character data. You will find that many programs are
just expanded versions of the prototypes that we discuss here.

Character Input and Output

The standard library provides functions for reading and writing a character at a time. getchar() fetches the *next input character* each time it is
called, and returns that character as its value. That is, after

```
c = getchar()
```

the variable c contains the next character of input. The characters normally
come from the terminal, but that need not concern us until Chapter 7.
The function putchar(c) is the complement of getchar:

```
putchar(c)
```

prints the contents of variable c on some output medium, again usually the
terminal. Calls to putchar and printf may be interleaved; the output
will appear in the order in which the calls are made.
As with printf, there is nothing special about getchar and
putchar. They are not part of the C language, but they are universally
available.

File Copying

Given `getchar` and `putchar`, you can write a surprising amount of useful code without knowing anything more about I/O. The simplest example is a program which copies its input to its output one character at a time. In outline,

> *get a character*
> *while (character is not end of file signal)*
> > *output the character just read*
> > *get a new character*

Converting this into C gives

```
main()     /* copy input to output; 1st version */
{
    int c;

    c = getchar();
    while (c != EOF) {
        putchar(c);
        c = getchar();
    }
}
```

The relational operator `!=` means "not equal to."

The main problem is detecting the end of the input. By convention, `getchar` returns a value which is not a valid character when it encounters the end of the input; in this way, programs can detect when they run out of input. The only complication, a serious nuisance, is that there are *two* conventions in common use about what that end of file value really is. We have deferred the issue by using the symbolic name EOF for the value, whatever it might be. In practice, EOF will be either −1 or 0, so the program must be preceded by the appropriate one of

```
#define   EOF   -1
```

or

```
#define   EOF   0
```

in order to work properly. By using the symbolic constant EOF to represent the value that `getchar` returns when end of file occurs, we are assured that only one thing in the program depends on the specific numeric value.

We also declare `c` to be an `int`, not a `char`, so it can hold the value which `getchar` returns. As we shall see in Chapter 2, this value is actually an `int`, since it must be capable of representing EOF in addition to all possible `char`'s.

The program for copying would actually be written more concisely by experienced C programmers. In C, any assignment, such as

```
c = getchar()
```

can be used in an expression; its value is simply the value being assigned to the left hand side. If the assignment of a character to c is put inside the test part of a while, the file copy program can be written

```
main()     /* copy input to output; 2nd version */
{
        int c;

        while ((c = getchar()) != EOF)
                putchar(c);
}
```

The program gets a character, assigns it to c, and then tests whether the character was the end of file signal. If it was not, the body of the while is executed, printing the character. The while then repeats. When the end of the input is finally reached, the while terminates and so does main.

This version centralizes the input — there is now only one call to getchar — and shrinks the program. Nesting an assignment in a test is one of the places where C permits a valuable conciseness. (It's possible to get carried away and create impenetrable code, though, a tendency that we will try to curb.)

It's important to recognize that the parentheses around the assignment within the conditional are really necessary. The *precedence* of != is higher than that of =, which means that in the absence of parentheses the relational test != would be done before the assignment =. So the statement

```
c = getchar() != EOF
```

is equivalent to

```
c = (getchar() != EOF)
```

This has the undesired effect of setting c to 0 or 1, depending on whether or not the call of getchar encountered end of file. (More on this in Chapter 2.)

Character Counting

The next program counts characters; it is a small elaboration of the copy program.

```
main()      /* count characters in input */
{
      long nc;

      nc = 0;
      while (getchar() != EOF)
            ++nc;
      printf("%ld\n", nc);
}
```

The statement

```
++nc;
```

shows a new operator, ++, which means *increment by one.* You could write nc = nc + 1 but ++nc is more concise and often more efficient. There is a corresponding operator -- to decrement by 1. The operators ++ and -- can be either prefix operators (++nc) or postfix (nc++); these two forms have different values in expressions, as will be shown in Chapter 2, but ++nc and nc++ both increment nc. For the moment we will stick to prefix.

The character counting program accumulates its count in a long variable instead of an int. On a PDP-11 the maximum value of an int is 32767, and it would take relatively little input to overflow the counter if it were declared int; in Honeywell and IBM C, long and int are synonymous and much larger. The conversion specification %ld signals to printf that the corresponding argument is a long integer.

To cope with even bigger numbers, you can use a double (double length float). We will also use a for statement instead of a while, to illustrate an alternative way to write the loop.

```
main()      /* count characters in input */
{
      double nc;

      for (nc = 0; getchar() != EOF; ++nc)
            ;
      printf("%.0f\n", nc);
}
```

printf uses %f for both float and double; %.0f suppresses printing of the non-existent fraction part.

The body of the for loop here is *empty,* because all of the work is done in the test and re-initialization parts. But the grammatical rules of C require that a for statement have a body. The isolated semicolon, technically a *null statement,* is there to satisfy that requirement. We put it on a separate line to make it more visible.

Before we leave the character counting program, observe that if the input contains no characters, the `while` or `for` test fails on the very first call to `getchar`, and so the program produces zero, the right answer. This is an important observation. One of the nice things about `while` and `for` is that they test at the *top* of the loop, before proceeding with the body. If there is nothing to do, nothing is done, even if that means never going through the loop body. Programs should act intelligently when handed input like ''no characters.'' The `while` and `for` statements help ensure that they do reasonable things with boundary conditions.

Line Counting

The next program counts *lines* in its input. Input lines are assumed to be terminated by the newline character `\n` that has been religiously appended to every line written out.

```
main()      /* count lines in input */
{
    int c, nl;

    nl = 0;
    while ((c = getchar()) != EOF)
        if (c == '\n')
            ++nl;
    printf("%d\n", nl);
}
```

The body of the `while` now consists of an `if`, which in turn controls the increment `++nl`. The `if` statement tests the parenthesized condition, and if it is true, does the statement (or group of statements in braces) that follows. We have again indented to show what is controlled by what.

The double equals sign `==` is the C notation for ''is equal to'' (like Fortran's `.EQ.`). This symbol is used to distinguish the equality test from the single `=` used for assignment. Since assignment is about twice as frequent as equality testing in typical C programs, it's appropriate that the operator be half as long.

Any single character can be written between single quotes, to produce a value equal to the numerical value of the character in the machine's character set; this is called a *character constant*. So, for example, `'A'` is a character constant; in the ASCII character set its value is 65, the internal representation of the character `A`. Of course `'A'` is to be preferred over 65: its meaning is obvious, and it is independent of a particular character set.

The escape sequences used in character strings are also legal in character constants, so in tests and arithmetic expressions, `'\n'` stands for the value of the newline character. You should note carefully that `'\n'` is a single character, and in expressions is equivalent to a single integer; on the other hand, "\n" is a character string which happens to contain only one character. The topic of strings versus characters is discussed further in Chapter 2.

Exercise 1-6. Write a program to count blanks, tabs, and newlines. □

Exercise 1-7. Write a program to copy its input to its output, replacing each string of one or more blanks by a single blank. □

Exercise 1-8. Write a program to replace each tab by the three-character sequence >, *backspace*, –, which prints as **>**, and each backspace by the similar sequence **<**. This makes tabs and backspaces visible. □

Word Counting

The fourth in our series of useful programs counts lines, words, and characters, with the loose definition that a word is any sequence of characters that does not contain a blank, tab or newline. (This is a bare-bones version of the UNIX utility *wc*.)

```
#define   YES  1
#define   NO   0

main()    /* count lines, words, chars in input */
{
    int c, nl, nw, nc, inword;

    inword = NO;
    nl = nw = nc = 0;
    while ((c = getchar()) != EOF) {
        ++nc;
        if (c == '\n')
            ++nl;
        if (c == ' ' || c == '\n' || c == '\t')
            inword = NO;
        else if (inword == NO) {
            inword = YES;
            ++nw;
        }
    }
    printf("%d %d %d\n", nl, nw, nc);
}
```

Every time the program encounters the first character of a word, it counts it. The variable `inword` records whether the program is currently in a word or not; initially it is "not in a word," which is assigned the value `NO`. We prefer the symbolic constants `YES` and `NO` to the literal values 1 and 0 because they make the program more readable. Of course in a program as tiny as this, it makes little difference, but in larger programs, the increase in clarity is well worth the modest extra effort to write it this way originally. You'll also find that it's easier to make extensive changes in programs where numbers appear only as symbolic constants.

The line

```
nl = nw = nc = 0;
```

sets all three variables to zero. This is not a special case, but a consequence of the fact that an assignment has a value and assignments associate right to left. It's really as if we had written

```
nc = (nl = (nw = 0));
```

The operator | | means OR, so the line

```
if (c == ' ' || c == '\n' || c == '\t')
```

says "if c is a blank *or* c is a newline *or* c is a tab ...". (The escape sequence \t is a visible representation of the tab character.) There is a corresponding operator && for AND. Expressions connected by && or | | are evaluated left to right, and it is guaranteed that evaluation will stop as soon as the truth or falsehood is known. Thus if c contains a blank, there is no need to test whether it contains a newline or tab, so these tests are *not* made. This isn't particularly important here, but is very significant in more complicated situations, as we will soon see.

The example also shows the C else statement, which specifies an alternative action to be done if the condition part of an if statement is false. The general form is

```
if (expression)
        statement-1
else
        statement-2
```

One and only one of the two statements associated with an if-else is done. If the *expression* is true, *statement-1* is executed; if not, *statement-2* is executed. Each *statement* can in fact be quite complicated. In the word count program, the one after the else is an if that controls two statements in braces.

Exercise 1-9. How would you test the word count program? What are some boundaries? □

Exercise 1-10. Write a program which prints the words in its input, one per line. □

Exercise 1-11. Revise the word count program to use a better definition of "word," for example, a sequence of letters, digits and apostrophes that begins with a letter. □

1.6   Arrays

Let us write a program to count the number of occurrences of each digit, of white space characters (blank, tab, newline), and all other characters. This is artificial, of course, but it permits us to illustrate several aspects of C in one program.

There are twelve categories of input, so it is convenient to use an array to hold the number of occurrences of each digit, rather than ten individual variables. Here is one version of the program:

```
main()      /* count digits, white space, others */
{
    int  c, i, nwhite, nother;
    int  ndigit[10];

    nwhite = nother = 0;
    for (i = 0; i < 10; ++i)
        ndigit[i] = 0;

    while ((c = getchar()) != EOF)
        if (c >= '0' && c <= '9')
            ++ndigit[c-'0'];
        else if (c == ' ' || c == '\n' || c == '\t')
            ++nwhite;
        else
            ++nother;

    printf("digits =");
    for (i = 0; i < 10; ++i)
        printf(" %d", ndigit[i]);
    printf("\nwhite space = %d, other = %d\n",
        nwhite, nother);
}
```

The declaration

```
    int  ndigit[10];
```

declares ndigit to be an array of 10 integers. Array subscripts always start at zero in C (rather than 1 as in Fortran or PL/I), so the elements are ndigit[0], ndigit[1], ..., ndigit[9]. This is reflected in the for loops which initialize and print the array.

A subscript can be any integer expression, which of course includes integer variables like i, and integer constants.

This particular program relies heavily on the properties of the character representation of the digits. For example, the test

```
    if (c >= '0' && c <= '9') ...
```

determines whether the character in c is a digit. If it is, the numeric value of that digit is

```
c - '0'
```

This works only if '0', '1', etc., are positive and in increasing order, and if there is nothing but digits between '0' and '9'. Fortunately, this is true for all conventional character sets.

By definition, arithmetic involving char's and int's converts everything to int before proceeding, so char variables and constants are essentially identical to int's in arithmetic contexts. This is quite natural and convenient; for example, c - '0' is an integer expression with a value between 0 and 9 corresponding to the character '0' to '9' stored in c, and is thus a valid subscript for the array ndigit.

The decision as to whether a character is a digit, a white space, or something else is made with the sequence

```
if (c >= '0' && c <= '9')
      ++ndigit[c-'0'];
else if (c == ' ' || c == '\n' || c == '\t')
      ++nwhite;
else
      ++nother;
```

The pattern

```
if (condition)
      statement
else if (condition)
      statement
else
      statement
```

occurs frequently in programs as a way to express a multi-way decision. The code is simply read from the top until some *condition* is satisfied; at that point the corresponding *statement* part is executed, and the entire construction is finished. (Of course *statement* can be several statements enclosed in braces.) If none of the conditions is satisfied, the *statement* after the final else is executed if it is present. If the final else and *statement* are omitted (as in the word count program), no action takes place. There can be an arbitrary number of

```
else if (condition)
      statement
```

groups between the initial if and the final else. As a matter of style, it is advisable to format this construction as we have shown, so that long decisions do not march off the right side of the page.

The `switch` statement, to be discussed in Chapter 3, provides another way to write a multi-way branch that is particularly suitable when the condition being tested is simply whether some integer or character expression matches one of a set of constants. For contrast, we will present a `switch` version of this program in Chapter 3.

Exercise 1-12. Write a program to print a histogram of the lengths of words in its input. It is easiest to draw the histogram horizontally; a vertical orientation is more challenging. □

1.7   Functions

In C, a *function* is equivalent to a subroutine or function in Fortran, or a procedure in PL/I, Pascal, etc. A function provides a convenient way to encapsulate some computation in a black box, which can then be used without worrying about its innards. Functions are really the only way to cope with the potential complexity of large programs. With properly designed functions, it is possible to ignore *how* a job is done; knowing *what* is done is sufficient. C is designed to make the use of functions easy, convenient and efficient; you will often see a function only a few lines long called only once, just because it clarifies some piece of code.

So far we have used only functions like `printf`, `getchar` and `putchar` that have been provided for us; now it's time to write a few of our own. Since C has no exponentiation operator like the `**` of Fortran or PL/I, let us illustrate the mechanics of function definition by writing a function `power(m, n)` to raise an integer m to a positive integer power n. That is, the value of `power(2, 5)` is 32. This function certainly doesn't do the whole job of `**` since it handles only positive powers of small integers, but it's best to confuse only one issue at a time.

Here is the function `power` and a main program to exercise it, so you can see the whole structure at once.

```
main()     /* test power function */
{
    int i;

    for (i = 0; i < 10; ++i)
        printf("%d %d %d\n", i, power(2,i), power(-3,i));
}
```

```
    power(x, n)      /* raise x to n-th power; n > 0 */
    int x, n;
    {
         int i, p;

         p = 1;
         for (i = 1; i <= n; ++i)
              p = p * x;
         return(p);
    }
```

Each function has the same form:

name (*argument list, if any*)
argument declarations, if any
{
      declarations
      statements
}

The functions can appear in either order, and in one source file or in two. Of course if the source appears in two files, you will have to say more to compile and load it than if it all appears in one, but that is an operating system matter, not a language attribute. For the moment, we will assume that both functions are in the same file, so whatever you have learned about running C programs will not change.

The function power is called twice in the line

```
    printf("%d %d %d\n", i, power(2,i), power(-3,i));
```

Each call passes two arguments to power, which each time returns an integer to be formatted and printed. In an expression, power(2,i) is an integer just as 2 and i are. (Not all functions produce an integer value; we will take this up in Chapter 4.)

In power the arguments have to be declared appropriately so their types are known. This is done by the line

```
    int x, n;
```

that follows the function name. The argument declarations go between the argument list and the opening left brace; each declaration is terminated by a semicolon. The names used by power for its arguments are purely *local* to power, and not accessible to any other function: other routines can use the same names without conflict. This is also true of the variables i and p: the i in power is unrelated to the i in main.

The value that power computes is returned to main by the return statement, which is just as in PL/I. Any expression may occur within the parentheses. A function need not return a value; a return statement with no expression causes control, but no useful value, to be returned to the caller, as does "falling off the end" of a function by reaching the terminating right brace.

Exercise 1-13. Write a program to convert its input to lower case, using a function `lower(c)` which returns c if c is not a letter, and the lower case value of c if it is a letter. □

1.8   Arguments — Call by Value

One aspect of C functions may be unfamiliar to programmers who are used to other languages, particularly Fortran and PL/I. In C, all function arguments are passed "by value." This means that the called function is given the values of its arguments in temporary variables (actually on a stack) rather than their addresses. This leads to some different properties than are seen with "call by reference" languages like Fortran and PL/I, in which the called routine is handed the address of the argument, not its value.

The main distinction is that in C the called function *cannot* alter a variable in the calling function; it can only alter its private, temporary copy.

Call by value is an asset, however, not a liability. It usually leads to more compact programs with fewer extraneous variables, because arguments can be treated as conveniently initialized local variables in the called routine. For example, here is a version of `power` which makes use of this fact.

```
power(x, n)    /* raise x to n-th power; n>0; version 2 */
int x, n;
{
    int p;

    for (p = 1; n > 0; --n)
        p = p * x;
    return(p);
}
```

The argument n is used as a temporary variable, and is counted down until it becomes zero; there is no longer a need for the variable i. Whatever is done to n inside `power` has no effect on the argument that `power` was originally called with.

When necessary, it is possible to arrange for a function to modify a variable in a calling routine. The caller must provide the *address* of the variable to be set (technically a *pointer* to the variable), and the called function must declare the argument to be a pointer and reference the actual variable indirectly through it. We will cover this in detail in Chapter 5.

When the name of an array is used as an argument, the value passed to the function is actually the location or address of the beginning of the array. (There is *no* copying of array elements.) By subscripting this value, the function can access and alter any element of the array. This is the topic of the next section.

1.9 Character Arrays

Probably the most common type of array in C is the array of characters. To illustrate the use of character arrays, and functions to manipulate them, let's write a program which reads a set of lines and prints the longest. The basic outline is simple enough:

```
while (there's another line)
        if (it's longer than the previous longest)
                save it and its length
    print longest line
```

This outline makes it clear that the program divides naturally into pieces. One piece gets a new line, another tests it, another saves it, and the rest controls the process.

Since things divide so nicely, it would be well to write them that way too. Accordingly, let us first write a separate function `getline` to fetch the *next line* of input; this is a generalization of `getchar`. To make the function useful in other contexts, we'll try to make it as flexible as possible. At the minimum, `getline` has to return a signal about possible end of file; a more generally useful design would be to return the length of the line, or zero if end of file is encountered. Zero is never a valid line length since every line has at least one character; even a line containing only a newline has length 1.

When we find a line that is longer than the previous longest, it must be saved somewhere. This suggests a second function, `copy`, to copy the new line to a safe place.

Finally, we need a main program to control `getline` and `copy`. Here is the result.

```
#define   MAXLINE   1000 /* maximum input line size */

main()    /* find longest line */
{
      int  len; /* current line length */
      int  max; /* maximum length seen so far */
      char line[MAXLINE]; /* current input line */
      char save[MAXLINE]; /* longest line, saved */

      max = 0;
      while ((len = getline(line, MAXLINE)) > 0)
            if (len > max) {
                  max = len;
                  copy(line, save);
            }
      if (max > 0)    /* there was a line */
            printf("%s", save);
}

getline(s, lim)       /* get line into s, return length */
char s[];
int lim;
{
      int c, i;

      for (i=0; i<lim-1 && (c=getchar())!=EOF && c!='\n'; ++i)
            s[i] = c;
      if (c == '\n') {
            s[i] = c;
            ++i;
      }
      s[i] = '\0';
      return(i);
}

copy(s1, s2)   /* copy s1 to s2; assume s2 big enough */
char s1[], s2[];
{
      int i;

      i = 0;
      while ((s2[i] = s1[i]) != '\0')
            ++i;
}
```

main and getline communicate both through a pair of arguments and a returned value. In getline, the arguments are declared by the lines

```
char s[];
int lim;
```

which specify that the first argument is an array, and the second is an integer. The length of the array `s` is not specified in `getline` since it is determined in `main`. `getline` uses `return` to send a value back to the caller, just as the function `power` did. Some functions return a useful value; others, like `copy`, are only used for their effect and return no value.

   `getline` puts the character `\0` (the *null character,* whose value is zero) at the end of the array it is creating, to mark the end of the string of characters. This convention is also used by the C compiler: when a string constant like

```
"hello\n"
```

is written in a C program, the compiler creates an array of characters containing the characters of the string, and terminates it with a `\0` so that functions such as `printf` can detect the end:

The `%s` format specification in `printf` expects a string represented in this form. If you examine `copy`, you will discover that it too relies on the fact that its input argument `s1` is terminated by `\0`, and it copies this character onto the output argument `s2`. (All of this implies that `\0` is not a part of normal text.)

   It is worth mentioning in passing that even a program as small as this one presents some sticky design problems. For example, what should `main` do if it encounters a line which is bigger than its limit? `getline` works properly, in that it stops collecting when the array is full, even if no newline has been seen. By testing the length and the last character returned, `main` can determine whether the line was too long, and then cope as it wishes. In the interests of brevity, we have ignored the issue.

   There is no way for a user of `getline` to know in advance how long an input line might be, so `getline` checks for overflow. On the other hand, the user of `copy` already knows (or can find out) how big the strings are, so we have chosen not to add error checking to it.

Exercise 1-14. Revise the main routine of the longest-line program so it will correctly print the length of arbitrarily long input lines, and as much as possible of the text. □

Exercise 1-15. Write a program to print all lines that are longer than 80 characters. □

Exercise 1-16. Write a program to remove trailing blanks and tabs from each line of input, and to delete entirely blank lines. □

Exercise 1-17. Write a function `reverse(s)` which reverses the character string `s`. Use it to write a program which reverses its input a line at a time.
□

1.10 Scope; External Variables

The variables in `main` (`line`, `save`, etc.) are private or local to `main`; because they are declared within `main`, no other function can have direct access to them. The same is true of the variables in other functions; for example, the variable `i` in `getline` is unrelated to the `i` in `copy`. Each local variable in a routine comes into existence only when the function is called, and *disappears* when the function is exited. It is for this reason that such variables are usually known as *automatic* variables, following terminology in other languages. We will use the term automatic henceforth to refer to these dynamic local variables. (Chapter 4 discusses the `static` storage class, in which local variables do retain their values between function invocations.)

Because automatic variables come and go with function invocation, they do not retain their values from one call to the next, and must be explicitly set upon each entry. If they are not set, they will contain garbage.

As an alternative to automatic variables, it is possible to define variables which are *external* to all functions, that is, global variables which can be accessed by name by any function that cares to. (This mechanism is rather like Fortran COMMON or PL/I EXTERNAL.) Because external variables are globally accessible, they can be used instead of argument lists to communicate data between functions. Furthermore, because external variables remain in existence permanently, rather than appearing and disappearing as functions are called and exited, they retain their values even after the functions that set them are done.

An external variable has to be *defined* outside of any function; this allocates actual storage for it. The variable must also be *declared* in each function that wants to access it; this may be done either by an explicit `extern` declaration or implicitly by context. To make the discussion concrete, let us rewrite the longest-line program with `line`, `save` and `max` as external variables. This requires changing the calls, declarations, and bodies of all three functions.

```
#define    MAXLINE    1000 /* maximum input line size */

char line[MAXLINE]; /* input line */
char save[MAXLINE]; /* longest line saved here */
int  max; /* length of longest line seen so far */

main()     /* find longest line; specialized version */
{
    int len;
    extern int max;
    extern char save[];

    max = 0;
    while ((len = getline()) > 0)
        if (len > max) {
            max = len;
            copy();
        }
    if (max > 0)    /* there was a line */
        printf("%s", save);
}

getline() /* specialized version */
{
    int c, i;
    extern char line[];

    for (i = 0; i < MAXLINE-1
        && (c=getchar()) != EOF && c != '\n'; ++i)
            line[i] = c;
    if (c == '\n') {
        line[i] = c;
        ++i;
    }
    line[i] = '\0';
    return(i);
}
```

```
copy()     /* specialized version */
{
    int i;
    extern char line[], save[];

    i = 0;
    while ((save[i] = line[i]) != '\0')
        ++i;
}
```

The external variables in `main`, `getline` and `copy` are *defined* by the first lines of the example above, which state their type and cause storage to be allocated for them. Syntactically, external definitions are just like the declarations we have used previously, but since they occur outside of functions, the variables are external. Before a function can use an external variable, the name of the variable must be made known to the function. One way to do this is to write an `extern` *declaration* in the function; the declaration is the same as before except for the added keyword `extern`.

In certain circumstances, the `extern` declaration can be omitted: if the external definition of a variable occurs in the source file *before* its use in a particular function, then there is no need for an `extern` declaration in the function. The `extern` declarations in `main`, `getline` and `copy` are thus redundant. In fact, common practice is to place definitions of all external variables at the beginning of the source file, and then omit all `extern` declarations.

If the program is on several source files, and a variable is defined in, say, *file1* and used in *file2*, then an `extern` declaration is needed in *file2* to connect the two occurrences of the variable. This topic is discussed at length in Chapter 4.

You should note that we are using the words *declaration* and *definition* carefully when we refer to external variables in this section. "Definition" refers to the place where the variable is actually created or assigned storage; "declaration" refers to places where the nature of the variable is stated but no storage is allocated.

By the way, there is a tendency to make everything in sight an `extern` variable because it appears to simplify communications — argument lists are short and variables are always there when you want them. But external variables are always there even when you don't want them. This style of coding is fraught with peril since it leads to programs whose data connections are not at all obvious — variables can be changed in unexpected and even inadvertent ways, and the program is hard to modify if it becomes necessary. The second version of the longest-line program is inferior to the first, partly for these reasons, and partly because it destroys the generality of two quite useful functions by wiring into them the names of the variables they will manipulate.

Exercise 1-18. The test in the `for` statement of `getline` above is rather ungainly. Rewrite the program to make it clearer, but retain the same behavior at end of file or buffer overflow. Is this behavior the most reasonable? □

1.11 Summary

At this point we have covered what might be called the conventional core of C. With this handful of building blocks, it's possible to write useful programs of considerable size, and it would probably be a good idea if you paused long enough to do so. The exercises that follow are intended to give you suggestions for programs of somewhat greater complexity than the ones presented in this chapter.

After you have this much of C under control, it will be well worth your effort to read on, for the features covered in the next few chapters are where the power and expressiveness of the language begin to become apparent.

Exercise 1-19. Write a program `detab` which replaces tabs in the input with the proper number of blanks to space to the next tab stop. Assume a fixed set of tab stops, say every *n* positions. □

Exercise 1-20. Write the program `entab` which replaces strings of blanks by the minimum number of tabs and blanks to achieve the same spacing. Use the same tab stops as for `detab`. □

Exercise 1-21. Write a program to "fold" long input lines after the last non-blank character that occurs before the *n*-th column of input, where *n* is a parameter. Make sure your program does something intelligent with very long lines, and if there are no blanks or tabs before the specified column. □

Exercise 1-22. Write a program to remove all comments from a C program. Don't forget to handle quoted strings and character constants properly. □

Exercise 1-23. Write a program to check a C program for rudimentary syntax errors like unbalanced parentheses, brackets and braces. Don't forget about quotes, both single and double, and comments. (This program is hard if you do it in full generality.) □

TYPES, OPERATORS AND EXPRESSIONS

Variables and constants are the basic data objects manipulated in a program. Declarations list the variables to be used, and state what type they have and perhaps what their initial values are. Operators specify what is to be done to them. Expressions combine variables and constants to produce new values. These are the topics of this chapter.

2.1 Variable Names

Although we didn't come right out and say so, there are some restrictions on variable and symbolic constant names. Names are made up of letters and digits; the first character must be a letter. The underscore "_" counts as a letter; it is useful for improving the readability of long variable names. Upper and lower case are different; traditional C practice is to use lower case for variable names, and all upper case for symbolic constants.

Only the first eight characters of an internal name are significant, although more may be used. For external names such as function names and external variables, the number may be less than eight, because external names are used by various assemblers and loaders. Appendix A lists details. Furthermore, keywords like `if`, `else`, `int`, `float`, etc., are *reserved*: you can't use them as variable names. (They must be in lower case.)

Naturally it's wise to choose variable names that mean something, that are related to the purpose of the variable, and that are unlikely to get mixed up typographically.

2.2 Data Types and Sizes

There are only a few basic data types in C:

char   a single byte, capable of holding one character
          in the local character set.
int   an integer, typically reflecting the natural size
          of integers on the host machine.
float   single-precision floating point.
double   double-precision floating point.

In addition, there are a number of qualifiers which can be applied to int's: short, long, and unsigned. short and long refer to different sizes of integers. unsigned numbers obey the laws of arithmetic modulo 2^n, where n is the number of bits in an int; unsigned numbers are always positive. The declarations for the qualifiers look like

```
short int x;
long int y;
unsigned int z;
```

The word int can be omitted in such situations, and typically is.

The precision of these objects depends on the machine at hand; the table below shows some representative values.

	DEC PDP-11	Honeywell 6000	IBM 370	Interdata 8/32
	ASCII	ASCII	EBCDIC	ASCII
char	8 bits	9 bits	8 bits	8 bits
int	16	36	32	32
short	16	36	16	16
long	32	36	32	32
float	32	36	32	32
double	64	72	64	64

The intent is that short and long should provide different lengths of integers where practical; int will normally reflect the most "natural" size for a particular machine. As you can see, each compiler is free to interpret short and long as appropriate for its own hardware. About all you should count on is that short is no longer than long.

2.3 Constants

int and float constants have already been disposed of, except to note that the usual

```
123.456e-7
```

or

```
0.12E3
```

"scientific" notation for float's is also legal. Every floating point constant is taken to be `double`, so the "e" notation serves for both `float` and `double`.

Long constants are written in the style `123L`. An ordinary integer constant that is too long to fit in an `int` is also taken to be a `long`.

There is a notation for octal and hexadecimal constants: a leading `0` (zero) on an `int` constant implies octal; a leading `0x` or `0X` indicates hexadecimal. For example, decimal 31 can be written as `037` in octal and `0x1f` or `0X1F` in hex. Hexadecimal and octal constants may also be followed by L to make them `long`.

A *character constant* is a single character written within single quotes, as in `'x'`. The value of a character constant is the numeric value of the character in the machine's character set. For example, in the ASCII character set the character zero, or `'0'`, is 48, and in EBCDIC `'0'` is 240, both quite different from the numeric value 0. Writing `'0'` instead of a numeric value like 48 or 240 makes the program independent of the particular value. Character constants participate in numeric operations just as any other numbers, although they are most often used in comparisons with other characters. A later section treats conversion rules.

Certain non-graphic characters can be represented in character constants by escape sequences like \n (newline), \t (tab), \0 (null), \\ (backslash), \' (single quote), etc., which look like two characters, but are actually only one. In addition, an arbitrary byte-sized bit pattern can be generated by writing

> `'\ddd'`

where *ddd* is one to three octal digits, as in

```
#define    FORMFEED  '\014'    /* ASCII form feed */
```

The character constant `'\0'` represents the character with value zero. `'\0'` is often written instead of 0 to emphasize the character nature of some expression.

A *constant expression* is an expression that involves only constants. Such expressions are evaluated at compile time, rather than run time, and accordingly may be used in any place that a constant may be, as in

```
#define    MAXLINE   1000
char line[MAXLINE+1];
```

or

```
seconds = 60 * 60 * hours;
```

A *string constant* is a sequence of zero or more characters surrounded by double quotes, as in

```
"I am a string"
```

or

```
""    /* a null string */
```

The quotes are not part of the string, but serve only to delimit it. The same escape sequences used for character constants apply in strings; \" represents the double quote character.

Technically, a string is an array whose elements are single characters. The compiler automatically places the null character \0 at the end of each such string, so programs can conveniently find the end. This representation means that there is no real limit to how long a string can be, but programs have to scan one completely to determine its length. The physical storage required is one more location than the number of characters written between the quotes. The following function strlen(s) returns the length of a character string s, excluding the terminal \0.

```
strlen(s) /* return length of s */
char s[];
{
    int i;

    i = 0;
    while (s[i] != '\0')
        ++i;
    return(i);
}
```

Be careful to distinguish between a character constant and a string that contains a single character: 'x' is not the same as "x". The former is a single character, used to produce the numeric value of the letter x in the machine's character set. The latter is a character string that contains one character (the letter x) and a \0.

2.4 Declarations

All variables must be declared before use, although certain declarations can be made implicitly by context. A declaration specifies a type, and is followed by a list of one or more variables of that type, as in

```
int  lower, upper, step;
char c, line[1000];
```

Variables can be distributed among declarations in any fashion; the lists above could equally well be written as

```
int   lower;
int   upper;
int   step;
char  c;
char  line[1000];
```

This latter form takes more room, but is convenient for adding a comment to each declaration or for subsequent modifications.

Variables may also be initialized in their declaration, although there are some restrictions. If the name is followed by an equals sign and a constant, that serves as an initializer, as in

```
char backslash = '\\';
int  i = 0;
float eps = 1.0e-5;
```

If the variable in question is external or static, the initialization is done once only, conceptually before the program starts executing. Explicitly initialized automatic variables are initialized each time the function they are in is called. Automatic variables for which there is no explicit initializer have undefined (i.e., garbage) values. External and static variables are initialized to zero by default, but it is good style to state the initialization anyway.

We will discuss initialization further as new data types are introduced.

2.5 Arithmetic Operators

The binary arithmetic operators are +, −, *, /, and the modulus operator %. There is a unary −, but no unary +.

Integer division truncates any fractional part. The expression

```
x % y
```

produces the remainder when x is divided by y, and thus is zero when y divides x exactly. For example, a year is a leap year if it is divisible by 4 but not by 100, except that years divisible by 400 *are* leap years. Therefore

```
if (year % 4 == 0 && year % 100 != 0 || year % 400 == 0)
```
     it's a leap year
```
else
```
     it's not

The % operator cannot be applied to `float` or `double`.

The + and − operators have the same precedence, which is lower than the (identical) precedence of *, /, and %, which are in turn lower than unary minus. Arithmetic operators group left to right. (A table at the end of this chapter summarizes precedence and associativity for all operators.) The order of evaluation is not specified for associative and commutative operators like * and +; the compiler may rearrange a parenthesized computation involving one of these. Thus a+(b+c) can be evaluated as (a+b)+c. This rarely makes any difference, but if a particular order is required, explicit temporary variables must be used.

The action taken on overflow or underflow depends on the machine at hand.

2.6 Relational and Logical Operators

The relational operators are

```
>    >=    <    <=
```

They all have the same precedence. Just below them in precedence are the equality operators:

```
==    !=
```

which have the same precedence. Relationals have lower precedence than arithmetic operators, so expressions like `i < lim-1` are taken as `i < (lim-1)`, as would be expected.

More interesting are the logical connectives `&&` and `||`. Expressions connected by `&&` or `||` are evaluated left to right, and evaluation stops as soon as the truth or falsehood of the result is known. These properties are critical to writing programs that work. For example, here is a loop from the input function `getline` which we wrote in Chapter 1.

```
for (i=0; i<lim-1 && (c=getchar()) != '\n' && c != EOF; ++i)
    s[i] = c;
```

Clearly, before reading a new character it is necessary to check that there is room to store it in the array s, so the test `i<lim-1` *must* be made first. Not only that, but if this test fails, we must not go on and read another character.

Similarly, it would be unfortunate if c were tested against EOF before `getchar` was called: the call must occur before the character in c is tested.

The precedence of `&&` is greater than that of `||`, and both are lower than relational and equality operators, so expressions like

```
i<lim-1 && (c = getchar()) != '\n' && c != EOF
```

need no extra parentheses. But since the precedence of `!=` is higher than assignment, parentheses are needed in

```
(c = getchar()) != '\n'
```

to achieve the desired result.

The unary negation operator `!` converts a non-zero or true operand into 0, and a zero or false operand into 1. A common use of `!` is in constructions like

```
    if (!inword)
```

rather than

```
    if (inword == 0)
```

It's hard to generalize about which form is better. Constructions like
!inword read quite nicely ("if not in word"), but more complicated ones
can be hard to understand.

Exercise 2-1. Write a loop equivalent to the for loop above without using
&&. □

2.7 Type Conversions

When operands of different types appear in expressions, they are converted to a common type according to a small number of rules. In general,
the only conversions that happen automatically are those that make sense,
such as converting an integer to floating point in an expression like f + i.
Expressions that don't make sense, like using a float as a subscript, are
disallowed.

First, char's and int's may be freely intermixed in arithmetic expressions: every char in an expression is automatically converted to an int.
This permits considerable flexibility in certain kinds of character transformations. One is exemplified by the function atoi, which converts a string of
digits into its numeric equivalent.

```
atoi(s)    /* convert s to integer */
char s[];
{
    int i, n;

    n = 0;
    for (i = 0; s[i] >= '0' && s[i] <= '9'; ++i)
        n = 10 * n + s[i] - '0';
    return(n);
}
```

As we discussed in Chapter 1, the expression

```
    s[i] - '0'
```

gives the numeric value of the character stored in s[i] because the values
of '0', '1', etc., form a contiguous increasing positive sequence.

Another example of char to int conversion is the function lower
which maps a single character to lower case *for the ASCII character set only.*
If the character is not an upper case letter, lower returns it unchanged.

```
lower(c)    /* convert c to lower case; ASCII only */
int c;
{
    if (c >= 'A' && c <= 'Z')
        return(c + 'a' - 'A');
    else
        return(c);
}
```

This works for ASCII because corresponding upper case and lower case letters are a fixed distance apart as numeric values and each alphabet is contiguous — there is nothing but letters between *A* and *Z*. This latter observation is *not* true of the EBCDIC character set (IBM 360/370), so this code fails on such systems — it converts more than letters.

There is one subtle point about the conversion of characters to integers. The language does not specify whether variables of type char are signed or unsigned quantities. When a char is converted to an int, can it ever produce a *negative* integer? Unfortunately, this varies from machine to machine, reflecting differences in architecture. On some machines (PDP-11, for instance), a char whose leftmost bit is 1 will be converted to a negative integer ("sign extension"). On others, a char is promoted to an int by adding zeros at the left end, and thus is always positive.

The definition of C guarantees that any character in the machine's standard character set will never be negative, so these characters may be used freely in expressions as positive quantities. But arbitrary bit patterns stored in character variables may appear to be negative on some machines, yet positive on others.

The most common occurrence of this situation is when the value −1 is used for EOF. Consider the code

```
char c;

c = getchar();
if (c == EOF)
        . . .
```

On a machine which does not do sign extension, c is always positive because it is a char, yet EOF is negative. As a result, the test always fails. To avoid this, we have been careful to use int instead of char for any variable which holds a value returned by getchar.

The real reason for using int instead of char is not related to any questions of possible sign extension. It is simply that getchar must return all possible characters (so that it can be used to read arbitrary input) and, in addition, a distinct EOF value. Thus its value *cannot* be represented as a char, but must instead be stored as an int.

Another useful form of automatic type conversion is that relational expressions like i > j and logical expressions connected by && and | | are defined to have value 1 if true, and 0 if false. Thus the assignment

```
isdigit = c >= '0' && c <= '9';
```

sets isdigit to 1 if c is a digit, and to 0 if not. (In the test part of if, while, for, etc., "true" just means "non-zero.")

Implicit arithmetic conversions work much as expected. In general, if an operator like + or * which takes two operands (a "binary operator") has operands of different types, the "lower" type is *promoted* to the "higher" type before the operation proceeds. The result is of the higher type. More precisely, for each arithmetic operator, the following sequence of conversion rules is applied.

> char and short are converted to int, and float is converted to double.

> Then if either operand is double, the other is converted to double, and the result is double.

> Otherwise if either operand is long, the other is converted to long, and the result is long.

> Otherwise if either operand is unsigned, the other is converted to unsigned, and the result is unsigned.

> Otherwise the operands must be int, and the result is int.

Notice that all float's in an expression are converted to double; all floating point arithmetic in C is done in double precision.

Conversions take place across assignments; the value of the right side is converted to the type of the left, which is the type of the result. A character is converted to an integer, either by sign extension or not, as described above. The reverse operation, int to char, is well-behaved — excess high-order bits are simply discarded. Thus in

```
int   i;
char c;

i = c;
c = i;
```

the value of c is unchanged. This is true whether or not sign extension is involved.

If x is float and i is int, then

```
x = i
```

and

```
i = x
```

both cause conversions; `float` to `int` causes truncation of any fractional part. `double` is converted to `float` by rounding. Longer `int`'s are converted to shorter ones or to `char`'s by dropping the excess high-order bits.

Since a function argument is an expression, type conversions also take place when arguments are passed to functions: in particular, `char` and `short` become `int`, and `float` becomes `double`. This is why we have declared function arguments to be `int` and `double` even when the function is called with `char` and `float`.

Finally, explicit type conversions can be forced ("coerced") in any expression with a construct called a *cast*. In the construction

(*type-name*) *expression*

the *expression* is converted to the named type by the conversion rules above. The precise meaning of a cast is in fact as if *expression* were assigned to a variable of the specified type, which is then used in place of the whole construction. For example, the library routine `sqrt` expects a `double` argument, and will produce nonsense if inadvertently handed something else. So if `n` is an integer,

```
sqrt((double) n)
```

converts `n` to `double` before passing it to `sqrt`. (Note that the cast produces the *value* of `n` in the proper type; the actual content of `n` is not altered.) The cast operator has the same precedence as other unary operators, as summarized in the table at the end of this chapter.

Exercise 2-2. Write the function `htoi(s)`, which converts a string of hexadecimal digits into its equivalent integer value. The allowable digits are 0 through 9, `a` through `f`, and `A` through `F`. □

2.8 Increment and Decrement Operators

C provides two unusual operators for incrementing and decrementing variables. The increment operator `++` adds 1 to its operand; the decrement operator `--` subtracts 1. We have frequently used `++` to increment variables, as in

```
if (c == '\n')
    ++nl;
```

The unusual aspect is that `++` and `--` may be used either as prefix operators (before the variable, as in `++n`), or postfix (after the variable: `n++`). In both cases, the effect is to increment n. But the expression `++n` increments n *before* using its value, while `n++` increments n *after* its value has been used. This means that in a context where the value is being used, not just the effect, ++n and n++ are different. If n is 5, then

```
x = n++;
```

sets x to 5, but

```
x = ++n;
```

sets x to 6. In both cases, n becomes 6. The increment and decrement operators can only be applied to variables; an expression like x=(i+j)++ is illegal.

In a context where no value is wanted, just the incrementing effect, as in

```
if (c == '\n')
     nl++;
```

choose prefix or postfix according to taste. But there are situations where one or the other is specifically called for. For instance, consider the function squeeze(s, c) which removes all occurrences of the character c from the string s.

```
squeeze(s, c)   /* delete all c from s */
char s[];
int c;
{
     int i, j;

     for (i = j = 0; s[i] != '\0'; i++)
          if (s[i] != c)
               s[j++] = s[i];
     s[j] = '\0';
}
```

Each time a non-c occurs, it is copied into the current j position, and only then is j incremented to be ready for the next character. This is exactly equivalent to

```
if (s[i] != c) {
     s[j] = s[i];
     j++;
}
```

Another example of a similar construction comes from the getline function which we wrote in Chapter 1, where we can replace

```
if (c == '\n') {
     s[i] = c;
     ++i;
}
```

by the more compact

```
if (c == '\n')
    s[i++] = c;
```

As a third example, the function strcat(s, t) concatenates the string t to the end of the string s. strcat assumes that there is enough space in s to hold the combination.

```
strcat(s, t)    /* concatenate t to end of s */
char s[], t[]; /* s must be big enough */
{
    int i, j;

    i = j = 0;
    while (s[i] != '\0')        /* find end of s */
        i++;
    while ((s[i++] = t[j++]) != '\0')   /* copy t */
        ;
}
```

As each character is copied from t to s, the postfix ++ is applied to both i and j to make sure that they are in position for the next pass through the loop.

Exercise 2-3. Write an alternate version of squeeze(s1, s2) which deletes each character in s1 which matches any character in the *string* s2. □

Exercise 2-4. Write the function any(s1, s2) which returns the first location in the string s1 where any character from the string s2 occurs, or −1 if s1 contains no characters from s2. □

2.9 Bitwise Logical Operators

C provides a number of operators for bit manipulation; these may not be applied to float or double.

&	bitwise AND
|	bitwise inclusive OR
^	bitwise exclusive OR
<<	left shift
>>	right shift
~	one's complement (unary)

The bitwise AND operator & is often used to mask off some set of bits; for example,

```
c = n & 0177;
```

sets to zero all but the low-order 7 bits of n. The bitwise OR operator | is used to turn bits on:

```
    x = x | MASK;
```

sets to one in x the bits that are set to one in MASK.

You should carefully distinguish the bitwise operators & and | from the logical connectives && and | |, which imply left-to-right evaluation of a truth value. For example, if x is 1 and y is 2, then x & y is zero while x && y is one. (Why?)

The shift operators << and >> perform left and right shifts of their left operand by the number of bit positions given by the right operand. Thus x << 2 shifts x left by two positions, filling vacated bits with 0; this is equivalent to multiplication by 4. Right shifting an unsigned quantity fills vacated bits with 0. Right shifting a signed quantity will fill with sign bits ("arithmetic shift") on some machines such as the PDP-11, and with 0-bits ("logical shift") on others.

The unary operator ~ yields the one's complement of an integer; that is, it converts each 1-bit into a 0-bit and vice versa. This operator typically finds use in expressions like

```
    x & ~077
```

which masks the last six bits of x to zero. Note that x & ~077 is independent of word length, and is thus preferable to, for example, x & 0177700, which assumes that x is a 16-bit quantity. The portable form involves no extra cost, since ~077 is a constant expression and thus evaluated at compile time.

To illustrate the use of some of the bit operators, consider the function getbits(x, p, n) which returns (right adjusted) the n-bit field of x that begins at position p. We assume that bit position 0 is at the right end and that n and p are sensible positive values. For example, getbits(x, 4, 3) returns the three bits in bit positions 4, 3 and 2, right adjusted.

```
    getbits(x, p, n)      /* get n bits from position p */
    unsigned x, p, n;
    {
        return((x >> (p+1-n)) & ~(~0 << n));
    }
```

x >> (p+1−n) moves the desired field to the right end of the word. Declaring the argument x to be unsigned ensures that when it is right-shifted, vacated bits will be filled with zeros, not sign bits, regardless of the machine the program is run on. ~0 is all 1-bits; shifting it left n bit positions with ~0 << n creates a mask with zeros in the rightmost n bits and ones everywhere else; complementing that with ~ makes a mask with ones in the rightmost n bits.

Exercise 2-5. Modify `getbits` to number bits from left to right. □

Exercise 2-6. Write a function `wordlength()` which computes the word length of the host machine, that is, the number of bits in an `int`. The function should be portable, in the sense that the same source code works on all machines. □

Exercise 2-7. Write the function `rightrot(n, b)` which rotates the integer `n` to the right by `b` bit positions. □

Exercise 2-8. Write the function `invert(x, p, n)` which inverts (i.e., changes 1 into 0 and vice versa) the `n` bits of `x` that begin at position `p`, leaving the others unchanged. □

2.10   Assignment Operators and Expressions

Expressions such as

```
i = i + 2
```

in which the left hand side is repeated on the right can be written in the compressed form

```
i += 2
```

using an *assignment operator* like +=.

Most binary operators (operators like + which have a left and right operand) have a corresponding assignment operator *op=*, where *op* is one of

```
+    -    *    /    %    <<    >>    &    ^    |
```

If *e1* and *e2* are expressions, then

> *e1 op= e2*

is equivalent to

> *e1 = (e1) op (e2)*

except that *e1* is computed only once. Notice the parentheses around *e2*:

```
x *= y + 1
```

is actually

```
x = x * (y + 1)
```

rather than

```
x = x * y + 1
```

As an example, the function `bitcount` counts the number of 1-bits in its integer argument.

```
bitcount(n)     /* count 1 bits in n */
unsigned n;
{
    int b;

    for (b = 0; n != 0; n >>= 1)
        if (n & 01)
            b++;
    return(b);
}
```

Quite apart from conciseness, assignment operators have the advantage that they correspond better to the way people think. We say "add 2 to i" or "increment i by 2," not "take i, add 2, then put the result back in i." Thus i += 2. In addition, for a complicated expression like

```
yyval[yypv[p3+p4] + yypv[p1+p2]] += 2
```

the assignment operator makes the code easier to understand, since the reader doesn't have to check painstakingly that two long expressions are indeed the same, or to wonder why they're not. And an assignment operator may even help the compiler to produce more efficient code.

We have already used the fact that the assignment statement has a value and can occur in expressions; the most common example is

```
while ((c = getchar()) != EOF)
    ...
```

Assignments using the other assignment operators (+=, -=, etc.) can also occur in expressions, although it is a less frequent occurrence.

The type of an assignment expression is the type of its left operand.

Exercise 2-9. In a 2's complement number system, x & (x-1) deletes the rightmost 1-bit in x. (Why?) Use this observation to write a faster version of bitcount. □

2.11 Conditional Expressions

The statements

```
if (a > b)
    z = a;
else
    z = b;
```

of course compute in z the maximum of a and b. The *conditional expression,* written with the ternary operator "?:", provides an alternate way to write this and similar constructions. In the expression *e1* ? *e2* : *e3*

the expression *e1* is evaluated first. If it is non-zero (true), then the expression *e2* is evaluated, and that is the value of the conditional expression. Otherwise *e3* is evaluated, and that is the value. Only one of *e2* and *e3* is evaluated. Thus to set z to the maximum of a and b,

```
z = (a > b) ? a : b;      /* z = max(a, b) */
```

It should be noted that the conditional expression is indeed an expression, and it can be used just as any other expression. If *e2* and *e3* are of different types, the type of the result is determined by the conversion rules discussed earlier in this chapter. For example, if f is a `float`, and n is an int, then the expression

```
(n > 0) ? f : n
```

is of type `double` regardless of whether n is positive or not.

Parentheses are not necessary around the first expression of a conditional expression, since the precedence of ?: is very low, just above assignment. They are advisable anyway, however, since they make the condition part of the expression easier to see.

The conditional expression often leads to succinct code. For example, this loop prints N elements of an array, 10 per line, with each column separated by one blank, and with each line (including the last) terminated by exactly one newline.

```
for (i = 0; i < N; i++)
    printf("%6d%c", a[i], (i%10==9 || i==N-1) ? '\n' : ' ');
```

A newline is printed after every tenth element, and after the N-th. All other elements are followed by one blank. Although this might look tricky, it's instructive to try to write it without the conditional expression.

Exercise 2-10. Rewrite the function `lower`, which converts upper case letters to lower case, with a conditional expression instead of `if-else`. □

2.12   Precedence and Order of Evaluation

The table below summarizes the rules for precedence and associativity of all operators, including those which we have not yet discussed. Operators on the same line have the same precedence; rows are in order of decreasing precedence, so, for example, *, /, and % all have the same precedence, which is higher than that of + and −.

Operator	Associativity
() [] -> .	left to right
! ~ ++ -- - (*type*) * & sizeof	right to left
* / %	left to right
+ -	left to right
<< >>	left to right
< <= > >=	left to right
== !=	left to right
&	left to right
^	left to right
|	left to right
&&	left to right
||	left to right
?:	right to left
= += -= etc.	right to left
, (Chapter 3)	left to right

The operators -> and . are used to access members of structures; they will be covered in Chapter 6, along with sizeof (size of an object). Chapter 5 discusses * (indirection) and & (address of).

Note that the precedence of the bitwise logical operators &, ^ and | falls below == and !=. This implies that bit-testing expressions like

```
    if ((x & MASK) == 0) ...
```

must be fully parenthesized to give proper results.

As mentioned before, expressions involving one of the associative and commutative operators (*, +, &, ^, |) can be rearranged even when parenthesized. In most cases this makes no difference whatsoever; in situations where it might, explicit temporary variables can be used to force a particular order of evaluation.

C, like most languages, does not specify in what order the operands of an operator are evaluated. For example, in a statement like

```
    x = f() + g();
```

f may be evaluated before g or vice versa; thus if either f or g alters an external variable that the other depends on, x can depend on the order of evaluation. Again, intermediate results can be stored in temporary variables to ensure a particular sequence.

Similarly, the order in which function arguments are evaluated is not specified, so the statement

```
printf("%d %d\n", ++n, power(2, n));    /* WRONG */
```

can (and does) produce different results on different machines, depending on whether or not n is incremented before power is called. The solution, of course, is to write

```
++n;
printf("%d %d\n", n, power(2, n));
```

Function calls, nested assignment statements, and increment and decrement operators cause "side effects" — some variable is changed as a by-product of the evaluation of an expression. In any expression involving side effects, there can be subtle dependencies on the order in which variables taking part in the expression are stored. One unhappy situation is typified by the statement

```
a[i] = i++;
```

The question is whether the subscript is the old value of i or the new. The compiler can do this in different ways, and generate different answers depending on its interpretation. When side effects (assignment to actual variables) takes place is left to the discretion of the compiler, since the best order strongly depends on machine architecture.

The moral of this discussion is that writing code which depends on order of evaluation is a bad programming practice in any language. Naturally, it is necessary to know what things to avoid, but if you don't know *how* they are done on various machines, that innocence may help to protect you. (The C verifier *lint* will detect most dependencies on order of evaluation.)

The control flow statements of a language specify the order in which computations are done. We have already met the most common control flow constructions of C in earlier examples; here we will complete the set, and be more precise about the ones discussed before.

3.1 Statements and Blocks

An *expression* such as `x = 0` or `i++` or `printf(...)` becomes a *statement* when it is followed by a semicolon, as in

```
x = 0;
i++;
printf(...);
```

In C, the semicolon is a statement terminator, rather than a separator as it is in Algol-like languages.

The braces { and } are used to group declarations and statements together into a *compound statement* or *block* so that they are syntactically equivalent to a single statement. The braces that surround the statements of a function are one obvious example; braces around multiple statements after an `if`, `else`, `while` or `for` are another. (Variables can actually be declared inside *any* block; we will talk about this in Chapter 4.) There is never a semicolon after the right brace that ends a block.

3.2 If-Else

The `if-else` statement is used to make decisions. Formally, the syntax is

```
if (expression)
    statement-1
else
    statement-2
```

where the `else` part is optional. The *expression* is evaluated; if it is "true"

51

(that is, if *expression* has a non-zero value), *statement-1* is done. If it is "false" (*expression* is zero) and if there is an `else` part, *statement-2* is executed instead.

Since an `if` simply tests the numeric value of an expression, certain coding shortcuts are possible. The most obvious is writing

```
if (expression)
```

instead of

```
if (expression != 0)
```

Sometimes this is natural and clear; at other times it is cryptic.

Because the `else` part of an `if-else` is optional, there is an ambiguity when an `else` is omitted from a nested `if` sequence. This is resolved in the usual way — the `else` is associated with the closest previous `else`-less `if`. For example, in

```
if (n > 0)
    if (a > b)
        z = a;
    else
        z = b;
```

the `else` goes with the inner `if`, as we have shown by indentation. If that isn't what you want, braces must be used to force the proper association:

```
if (n > 0) {
    if (a > b)
        z = a;
}
else
    z = b;
```

The ambiguity is especially pernicious in situations like:

```
if (n > 0)
    for (i = 0; i < n; i++)
        if (s[i] > 0) {
            printf("...");
            return(i);
        }
else        /* WRONG */
    printf("error - n is zero\n");
```

The indentation shows unequivocally what you want, but the compiler doesn't get the message, and associates the `else` with the inner `if`. This kind of bug can be very hard to find.

By the way, notice that there is a semicolon after `z = a` in

```
if (a > b)
    z = a;
else
    z = b;
```

This is because grammatically, a *statement* follows the `if`, and an expression statement like `z = a` is always terminated by a semicolon.

3.3   Else-If

The construction

```
if (expression)
    statement
else if (expression)
    statement
else if (expression)
    statement
else
    statement
```

occurs so often that it is worth a brief separate discussion. This sequence of `if`'s is the most general way of writing a multi-way decision. The *expression*'s are evaluated in order; if any *expression* is true, the *statement* associated with it is executed, and this terminates the whole chain. The code for each *statement* is either a single statement, or a group in braces.

The last `else` part handles the "none of the above" or default case where none of the other conditions was satisfied. Sometimes there is no explicit action for the default; in that case the trailing

```
else
    statement
```

can be omitted, or it may be used for error checking to catch an "impossible" condition.

To illustrate a three-way decision, here is a binary search function that decides if a particular value x occurs in the sorted array v. The elements of v must be in increasing order. The function returns the position (a number between 0 and n–1) if x occurs in v, and –1 if not.

```
binary(x, v, n)        /* find x in v[0] ... v[n-1] */
int x, v[], n;
{
    int low, high, mid;

    low = 0;
    high = n - 1;
    while (low <= high) {
        mid = (low+high) / 2;
        if (x < v[mid])
            high = mid - 1;
        else if (x > v[mid])
            low = mid + 1;
        else /* found match */
            return(mid);
    }
    return(-1);
}
```

The fundamental decision is whether x is less than, greater than, or equal to the middle element v[mid] at each step; this is a natural for else-if.

3.4   Switch

The switch statement is a special multi-way decision maker that tests whether an expression matches one of a number of *constant* values, and branches accordingly. In Chapter 1 we wrote a program to count the occurrences of each digit, white space, and all other characters, using a sequence of if ... else if ... else. Here is the same program with a switch.

```
main()      /* count digits, white space, others */
{
    int c, i, nwhite, nother, ndigit[10];

    nwhite = nother = 0;
    for (i = 0; i < 10; i++)
        ndigit[i] = 0;

    while ((c = getchar()) != EOF)
        switch (c) {
        case '0':
        case '1':
        case '2':
        case '3':
        case '4':
        case '5':
        case '6':
        case '7':
        case '8':
        case '9':
            ndigit[c-'0']++;
            break;
        case ' ':
        case '\n':
        case '\t':
            nwhite++;
            break;
        default:
            nother++;
            break;
        }

    printf("digits =");
    for (i = 0; i < 10; i++)
        printf(" %d", ndigit[i]);
    printf("\nwhite space = %d, other = %d\n",
        nwhite, nother);
}
```

The switch evaluates the integer expression in parentheses (in this program the character c) and compares its value to all the cases. Each case must be labeled by an integer or character constant or constant expression. If a case matches the expression value, execution starts at that case. The case labeled default is executed if none of the other cases is satisfied. A default is optional; if it isn't there and if none of the cases matches, no action at all takes place. Cases and default can occur in any order. Cases must all be different.

The `break` statement causes an immediate exit from the `switch`. Because cases serve just as labels, after the code for one case is done, execution *falls through* to the next unless you take explicit action to escape. `break` and `return` are the most common ways to leave a `switch`. A `break` statement can also be used to force an immediate exit from `while`, `for` and `do` loops as well, as will be discussed later in this chapter.

Falling through cases is a mixed blessing. On the positive side, it allows multiple cases for a single action, as with the blank, tab or newline in this example. But it also implies that normally each case must end with a `break` to prevent falling through to the next. Falling through from one case to another is not robust, being prone to disintegration when the program is modified. With the exception of multiple labels for a single computation, fall-throughs should be used sparingly.

As a matter of good form, put a `break` after the last case (the `default` here) even though it's logically unnecessary. Some day when another case gets added at the end, this bit of defensive programming will save you.

Exercise 3-1. Write a function `expand(s, t)` which converts characters like newline and tab into visible escape sequences like \n and \t as it copies the string `s` to `t`. Use a `switch`. □

3.5 Loops — While and For

We have already encountered the `while` and `for` loops. In

```
while (expression)
    statement
```

the *expression* is evaluated. If it is non-zero, *statement* is executed and *expression* is re-evaluated. This cycle continues until *expression* becomes zero, at which point execution resumes after *statement*.

The `for` statement

```
for (expr1 ; expr2 ; expr3)
    statement
```

is equivalent to

```
expr1 ;
while (expr2) {
    statement
    expr3 ;
}
```

Grammatically, the three components of a `for` are expressions. Most commonly, *expr1* and *expr3* are assignments or function calls and *expr2* is a relational expression. Any of the three parts can be omitted, although the semicolons must remain. If *expr1* or *expr3* is left out, i is simply dropped from the expansion. If the test, *expr2*, is not present, it is taken as permanently true, so

```
for (;;) {
    ...
}
```

is an "infinite" loop, presumably to be broken by other means (such as a `break` or `return`).

Whether to use `while` or `for` is largely a matter of taste. For example, in

```
while ((c = getchar()) == ' ' || c == '\n' || c == '\t')
    ;     /* skip white space characters */
```

there is no initialization or re-initialization, so the `while` seems most natural.

The `for` is clearly superior when there is a simple initialization and re-initialization, since it keeps the loop control statements close together and visible at the top of the loop. This is most obvious in

```
for (i = 0; i < N; i++)
```

which is the C idiom for processing the first N elements of an array, the analog of the Fortran or PL/I DO loop. The analogy is not perfect, however, since the limits of a `for` loop can be altered from within the loop, and the controlling variable i retains its value when the loop terminates for any reason. Because the components of the `for` are arbitrary expressions, `for` loops are not restricted to arithmetic progressions. Nonetheless, it is bad style to force unrelated computations into a `for`; it is better reserved for loop control operations.

As a larger example, here is another version of `atoi` for converting a string to its numeric equivalent. This one is more general; it copes with optional leading white space and an optional + or − sign. (Chapter 4 shows `atof`, which does the same conversion for floating point numbers.)

The basic structure of the program reflects the form of the input:

> *skip white space, if any*
> *get sign, if any*
> *get integer part, convert it*

Each step does its part, and leaves things in a clean state for the next. The whole process terminates on the first character that could not be part of a number.

```
atoi(s)     /* convert s to integer */
char s[];
{
    int i, n, sign;

    for (i=0; s[i]==' ' || s[i]=='\n' || s[i]=='\t'; i++)
        ;       /* skip white space */
    sign = 1;
    if (s[i] == '+' || s[i] == '-')     /* sign */
        sign = (s[i++]=='+') ? 1 : -1;
    for (n = 0; s[i] >= '0' && s[i] <= '9'; i++)
        n = 10 * n + s[i] - '0';
    return(sign * n);
}
```

The advantages of keeping loop control centralized are even more obvious when there are several nested loops. The following function is a Shell sort for sorting an array of integers. The basic idea of the Shell sort is that in early stages, far-apart elements are compared, rather than adjacent ones, as in simple interchange sorts. This tends to eliminate large amounts of disorder quickly, so later stages have less work to do. The interval between compared elements is gradually decreased to one, at which point the sort effectively becomes an adjacent interchange method.

```
shell(v, n)   /* sort v[0]...v[n-1] into increasing order */
int v[], n;
{
    int gap, i, j, temp;

    for (gap = n/2; gap > 0; gap /= 2)
        for (i = gap; i < n; i++)
            for (j=i-gap; j>=0 && v[j]>v[j+gap]; j-=gap) {
                temp = v[j];
                v[j] = v[j+gap];
                v[j+gap] = temp;
            }
}
```

There are three nested loops. The outermost loop controls the gap between compared elements, shrinking it from n/2 by a factor of two each pass until it becomes zero. The middle loop compares each pair of elements that is separated by gap; the innermost loop reverses any that are out of order. Since gap is eventually reduced to one, all elements are eventually ordered correctly. Notice that the generality of the for makes the outer loop fit the same form as the others, even though it is not an arithmetic progression.

One final C operator is the comma ",", which most often finds use in the for statement. A pair of expressions separated by a comma is evaluated left to right, and the type and value of the result are the type and value of the right operand. Thus in a `for` statement, it is possible to place multiple expressions in the various parts, for example to process two indices in parallel. This is illustrated in the function `reverse(s)`, which reverses the string `s` in place.

```
reverse(s)        /* reverse string s in place */
char s[];
{
      int c, i, j;

      for (i = 0, j = strlen(s)-1; i < j; i++, j--) {
            c = s[i];
            s[i] = s[j];
            s[j] = c;
      }
}
```

The commas that separate function arguments, variables in declarations, etc., are *not* comma operators, and do *not* guarantee left to right evaluation.

Exercise 3-2. Write a function `expand(s1, s2)` which expands short-hand notations like `a-z` in the string `s1` into the equivalent complete list `abc...xyz` in `s2`. Allow for letters of either case and digits, and be prepared to handle cases like `a-b-c` and `a-z0-9` and `-a-z`. (A useful convention is that a leading or trailing `-` is taken literally.) □

3.6 Loops — Do-while

The `while` and `for` loops share the desirable attribute of testing the termination condition at the top, rather than at the bottom, as we discussed in Chapter 1. The third loop in C, the `do-while`, tests at the bottom *after* making each pass through the loop body; the body is always executed at least once. The syntax is

```
do
      statement
while (expression);
```

The *statement* is executed, then *expression* is evaluated. If it is true, *statement* is evaluated again, and so on. If the expression becomes false, the loop terminates.

As might be expected, `do-while` is much less used than `while` and `for`, accounting for perhaps five percent of all loops. Nonetheless, it is from time to time valuable, as in the following function `itoa`, which converts a number to a character string (the inverse of `atoi`). The job is slightly more complicated than might be thought at first, because the easy

methods of generating the digits generate them in the wrong order. We
have chosen to generate the string backwards, then reverse it.

```
itoa(n, s)      /* convert n to characters in s */
char s[];
int n;
{
    int i, sign;

    if ((sign = n) < 0) /* record sign */
        n = -n;          /* make n positive */
    i = 0;
    do {        /* generate digits in reverse order */
        s[i++] = n % 10 + '0';   /* get next digit */
    } while ((n /= 10) > 0); /* delete it */
    if (sign < 0)
        s[i++] = '-';
    s[i] = '\0';
    reverse(s);
}
```

The do-while is necessary, or at least convenient, since at least one character must be installed in the array s, regardless of the value of n. We also
used braces around the single statement that makes up the body of the
do-while, even though they are unnecessary, so the hasty reader will not
mistake the while part for the *beginning* of a while loop.

Exercise 3-3. In a 2's complement number representation, our version of
itoa does not handle the largest negative number, that is, the value of *n*
equal to $-(2^{wordsize-1})$. Explain why not. Modify it to print that value
correctly, regardless of the machine it runs on. □

Exercise 3-4. Write the analogous function itob(n, s) which converts
the unsigned integer n into a binary character representation in s. Write
itoh, which converts an integer to hexadecimal representation. □

Exercise 3-5. Write a version of itoa which accepts three arguments
instead of two. The third argument is a minimum field width; the converted
number must be padded with blanks on the left if necessary to make it wide
enough. □

3.7 Break

It is sometimes convenient to be able to control loop exits other than by testing at the top or bottom. The `break` statement provides an early exit from `for`, `while`, and `do`, just as from `switch`. A `break` statement causes the innermost enclosing loop (or `switch`) to be exited immediately.

The following program removes trailing blanks and tabs from the end of each line of input, using a `break` to exit from a loop when the rightmost non-blank, non-tab is found.

```
#define    MAXLINE    1000

main()     /* remove trailing blanks and tabs */
{
      int   n;
      char  line[MAXLINE];

      while ((n = getline(line, MAXLINE)) > 0) {
            while (--n >= 0)
                  if (line[n] != ' ' && line[n] != '\t'
                      && line[n] != '\n')
                        break;
            line[n+1] = '\0';
            printf("%s\n", line);
      }
}
```

`getline` returns the length of the line. The inner `while` loop starts at the last character of `line` (recall that `--n` decrements n before using the value), and scans backwards looking for the first character that is not a blank, tab or newline. The loop is broken when one is found, or when n becomes negative (that is, when the entire line has been scanned). You should verify that this is correct behavior even when the line contains only white space characters.

An alternative to `break` is to put the testing in the loop itself:

```
while ((n = getline(line, MAXLINE)) > 0) {
      while (--n >= 0
         && (line[n]==' ' || line[n]=='\t' || line[n]=='\n'))
               ;
      ...
}
```

This is inferior to the previous version, because the test is harder to understand. Tests which require a mixture of `&&`, `||`, `!`, or parentheses should generally be avoided.

3.8   Continue

The `continue` statement is related to `break`, but less often used; it causes the *next iteration* of the enclosing loop (`for`, `while`, `do`) to begin. In the `while` and `do`, this means that the test part is executed immediately; in the `for`, control passes to the re-initialization step. (`continue` applies only to loops, not to `switch`. A `continue` inside a `switch` inside a loop causes the next loop iteration.)

As an example, this fragment processes only positive elements in the array `a`; negative values are skipped.

```
for (i = 0; i < N; i++) {
    if (a[i] < 0)   /* skip negative elements */
        continue;
    ... /* do positive elements */
}
```

The `continue` statement is often used when the part of the loop that follows is complicated, so that reversing a test and indenting another level would nest the program too deeply.

Exercise 3-6. Write a program which copies its input to its output, except that it prints only one instance from each group of adjacent identical lines. (This is a simple version of the UNIX utility *uniq*.) □

3.9   Goto's and Labels

C provides the infinitely-abusable `goto` statement, and labels to branch to. Formally, the `goto` is never necessary, and in practice it is almost always easy to write code without it. We have not used `goto` in this book.

Nonetheless, we will suggest a few situations where `goto`'s may find a place. The most common use is to abandon processing in some deeply nested structure, such as breaking out of two loops at once. The `break` statement cannot be used directly since it leaves only the innermost loop. Thus:

```
for ( ... )
    for ( ... ) {
        ...
        if (disaster)
            goto error;
    }
    ...

error:
        clean up the mess
```

This organization is handy if the error-handling code is non-trivial, and if

errors can occur in several places. A label has the same form as a variable
name, and is followed by a colon. It can be attached to any statement in the
same function as the goto.

As another example, consider the problem of finding the first negative
element in a two-dimensional array. (Multi-dimensional arrays are discussed
in Chapter 5.) One possibility is

```
        for (i = 0; i < N; i++)
            for (j = 0; j < M; j++)
                if (v[i][j] < 0)
                    goto found;
    /* didn't find */
    ...
found:
    /* found one at position i, j */
    ...
```

Code involving a goto can always be written without one, though
perhaps at the price of some repeated tests or an extra variable. For example, the array search becomes

```
    found = 0;
    for (i = 0; i < N && !found; i++)
        for (j = 0; j < M && !found; j++)
            found = v[i][j] < 0;
    if (found)
        /* it was at i-1, j-1 */
        ...
    else
        /* not found */
        ...
```

Although we are not dogmatic about the matter, it does seem that goto
statements should be used sparingly, if at all.

CHAPTER 4

FUNCTIONS AND PROGRAM STRUCTURE

Functions break large computing tasks into smaller ones, and enable people to build on what others have done instead of starting over from scratch. Appropriate functions can often hide details of operation from parts of the program that don't need to know about them, thus clarifying the whole, and easing the pain of making changes.

C has been designed to make functions efficient and easy to use; C programs generally consist of numerous small functions rather than a few big ones. A program may reside on one or more source files in any convenient way; the source files may be compiled separately and loaded together, along with previously compiled functions from libraries. We will not go into that process here, since the details vary according to the local system.

Most programmers are familiar with "library" functions for input and output (`getchar`, `putchar`) and numerical computations (`sin`, `cos`, `sqrt`). In this chapter we will show more about writing new functions.

4.1 Basics

To begin, let us design and write a program to print each line of its input that contains a particular "pattern" or string of characters. (This is a special case of the UNIX utility program *grep.*) For example, searching for the pattern "the" in the set of lines

        Now is the time
        for all good
        men to come to the aid
        of their party.

will produce the output

        Now is the time
        men to come to the aid
        of their party.

The basic structure of the job falls neatly into three pieces:

65

```
while  (there's another line)
    if  (the line contains the pattern)
        print it
```

Although it's certainly possible to put the code for all of this in the main routine, a better way is to use the natural structure to advantage by making each part a separate function. Three small pieces are easier to deal with than one big one, because irrelevant details can be buried in the functions, and the chance of unwanted interactions minimized. And the pieces may even be useful in their own right.

"While there's another line" is `getline`, a function that we wrote in Chapter 1, and "print it" is `printf`, which someone has already provided for us. This means we need only write a routine which decides if the line contains an occurrence of the pattern. We can solve that problem by stealing a design from PL/I: the function `index(s, t)` returns the position or index in the string `s` where the string `t` begins, or −1 if `s` doesn't contain `t`. We use 0 rather than 1 as the starting position in `s` because C arrays begin at position zero. When we later need more sophisticated pattern matching we only have to replace `index`; the rest of the code can remain the same.

Given this much design, filling in the details of the program is straightforward. Here is the whole thing, so you can see how the pieces fit together. For now, the pattern to be searched for is a literal string in the argument of `index`, which is not the most general of mechanisms. We will return shortly to a discussion of how to initialize character arrays, and in Chapter 5 will show how to make the pattern a parameter that is set when the program is run. This is also a new version of `getline`; you might find it instructive to compare it to the one in Chapter 1.

```
#define   MAXLINE   1000

main()    /* find all lines matching a pattern */
{
    char line[MAXLINE];

    while (getline(line, MAXLINE) > 0)
        if (index(line, "the") >= 0)
            printf("%s", line);
}
```

```
getline(s, lim)      /* get line into s, return length */
char s[];
int lim;
{
    int c, i;

    i = 0;
    while (--lim > 0 && (c=getchar()) != EOF && c != '\n')
        s[i++] = c;
    if (c == '\n')
        s[i++] = c;
    s[i] = '\0';
    return(i);
}


index(s, t)     /* return index of t in s, -1 if none */
char s[], t[];
{
    int i, j, k;

    for (i = 0; s[i] != '\0'; i++) {
        for (j=i, k=0; t[k]!='\0' && s[j]==t[k]; j++, k++)
            ;
        if (t[k] == '\0')
            return(i);
    }
    return(-1);
}
```

Each function has the form

name (argument list, if any)
argument declarations, if any
{
    declarations and statements, if any
}

As suggested, the various parts may be absent; a minimal function is

```
dummy() {}
```

which does nothing. (A do-nothing function is sometimes useful as a place holder during program development.) The function name may also be pre-ceded by a type if the function returns something other than an integer value; this is the topic of the next section.

A program is just a set of individual function definitions. Communica-tion between the functions is (in this case) by arguments and values returned by the functions; it can also be via external variables. The func-tions can occur in any order on the source file, and the source program can be split into multiple files, so long as no function is split.

The `return` statement is the mechanism for returning a value from the called function to its caller. Any expression can follow `return`:

> `return` (*expression*)

The calling function is free to ignore the returned value if it wishes. Furthermore, there need be no expression after `return`; in that case, no value is returned to the caller. Control also returns to the caller with no value when execution "falls off the end" of the function by reaching the closing right brace. It is not illegal, but probably a sign of trouble, if a function returns a value from one place and no value from another. In any case, the "value" of a function which does not return one is certain to be garbage. The C verifier *lint* checks for such errors.

The mechanics of how to compile and load a C program which resides on multiple source files vary from one system to the next. On the UNIX system, for example, the *cc* command mentioned in Chapter 1 does the job. Suppose that the three functions are on three files called *main.c*, *getline.c*, and *index.c*. Then the command

> *cc main.c getline.c index.c*

compiles the three files, places the resulting relocatable object code in files *main.o*, *getline.o*, and *index.o*, and loads them all into an executable file called *a.out*.

If there is an error, say in *main.c*, that file can be recompiled by itself and the result loaded with the previous object files, with the command

> *cc main.c getline.o index.o*

The *cc* command uses the ".*c*" versus ".*o*" naming convention to distinguish source files from object files.

Exercise 4-1. Write the function `rindex(s, t)`, which returns the position of the *rightmost* occurrence of t in s, or −1 if there is none. □

4.2   Functions Returning Non-Integers

So far, none of our programs has contained any declaration of the type of a function. This is because by default a function is implicitly declared by its appearance in an expression or statement, such as

> `while (getline(line, MAXLINE) > 0)`

If a name which has not been previously declared occurs in an expression and is followed by a left parenthesis, it is declared by context to be a function name. Furthermore, by default the function is assumed to return an `int`. Since `char` promotes to `int` in expressions, there is no need to declare functions that return `char`. These assumptions cover the majority of cases, including all of our examples so far.

But what happens if a function must return some other type? Many numerical functions like sqrt, sin, and cos return double; other specialized functions return other types. To illustrate how to deal with this, let us write and use the function atof(s), which converts the string s to its double-precision floating point equivalent. atof is an extension of atoi, which we wrote versions of in Chapters 2 and 3; it handles an optional sign and decimal point, and the presence or absence of either integer part or fractional part. (This is *not* a high-quality input conversion routine; that would take more space than we care to use.)

First, atof itself must declare the type of value it returns, since it is not int. Because float is converted to double in expressions, there is no point to saying that atof returns float; we might as well make use of the extra precision and thus we declare it to return double. The type name precedes the function name, like this:

```
double atof(s)  /* convert string s to double */
char s[];
{
    double val, power;
    int  i, sign;

    for (i=0; s[i]==' ' || s[i]=='\n' || s[i]=='\t'; i++)
        ;               /* skip white space */
    sign = 1;
    if (s[i] == '+' || s[i] == '-')     /* sign */
        sign = (s[i++]=='+') ? 1 : -1;
    for (val = 0; s[i] >= '0' && s[i] <= '9'; i++)
        val = 10 * val + s[i] - '0';
    if (s[i] == '.')
        i++;
    for (power = 1; s[i] >= '0' && s[i] <= '9'; i++) {
        val = 10 * val + s[i] - '0';
        power *= 10;
    }
    return(sign * val / power);
}
```

Second, and just as important, the *calling* routine must state that atof returns a non-int value. The declaration is shown in the following primitive desk calculator (barely adequate for check-book balancing), which reads one number per line, optionally preceded by a sign, and adds them all up, printing the sum after each input.

```
#define   MAXLINE   100

main()    /* rudimentary desk calculator */
{
      double sum, atof();
      char line[MAXLINE];

      sum = 0;
      while (getline(line, MAXLINE) > 0)
            printf("\t%.2f\n", sum += atof(line));
}
```

The declaration

```
double sum, atof();
```

says that `sum` is a `double` variable, and that `atof` is a function that returns a `double` value. As a mnemonic, it suggests that `sum` and `atof(...)` are both double-precision floating point values.

Unless `atof` is explicitly declared in both places, C assumes that it returns an integer, and you'll get nonsense answers. If `atof` itself and the call to it in `main` are typed inconsistently in the same source file, it will be detected by the compiler. But if (as is more likely) `atof` were compiled separately, the mismatch would not be detected, `atof` would return a `double` which `main` would treat as an `int`, and meaningless answers would result. (*lint* catches this error.)

Given `atof`, we could in principle write `atoi` (convert a string to `int`) in terms of it:

```
atoi(s)   /* convert string s to integer */
char s[];
{
      double atof();

      return(atof(s));
}
```

Notice the structure of the declarations and the `return` statement. The value of the expression in

```
return(expression)
```

is always converted to the type of the function before the return is taken. Therefore, the value of `atof`, a `double`, is converted automatically to `int` when it appears in a `return`, since the function `atoi` returns an `int`. (The conversion of a floating point value to `int` truncates any fractional part, as discussed in Chapter 2.)

Exercise 4-2. Extend `atof` so it handles scientific notation of the form

```
123.45e-6
```

where a floating point number may be followed by `e` or `E` and an optionally signed exponent. □

4.3 More on Function Arguments

In Chapter 1 we discussed the fact that function arguments are passed by value, that is, the called function receives a private, temporary copy of each argument, not its address. This means that the function cannot affect the original argument in the calling function. Within a function, each argument is in effect a local variable initialized to the value with which the function was called.

When an array name appears as an argument to a function, the location of the beginning of the array is passed; elements are not copied. The function can alter elements of the array by subscripting from this location. The effect is that arrays are passed by reference. In Chapter 5 we will discuss the use of pointers to permit functions to affect non-arrays in calling functions.

By the way, there is no entirely satisfactory way to write a portable function that accepts a variable number of arguments, because there is no portable way for the called function to determine how many arguments were actually passed to it in a given call. Thus, you can't write a truly portable function that will compute the maximum of an arbitrary number of arguments, as will the MAX built-in functions of Fortran and PL/I.

It is generally safe to deal with a variable number of arguments if the called function doesn't use an argument which was not actually supplied, and if the types are consistent. `printf`, the most common C function with a variable number of arguments, uses information from the first argument to determine how many other arguments are present and what their types are. It fails badly if the caller does not supply enough arguments or if the types are not what the first argument says. It is also non-portable and must be modified for different environments.

Alternatively, if the arguments are of known types it is possible to mark the end of the argument list in some agreed-upon way, such as a special argument value (often zero) that stands for the end of the arguments.

4.4   External Variables

A C program consists of a set of external objects, which are either variables or functions. The adjective "external" is used primarily in contrast to "internal," which describes the arguments and automatic variables defined inside functions. External variables are defined outside any function, and are thus potentially available to many functions. Functions themselves are always external, because C does not allow functions to be defined inside other functions. By default, external variables are also "global," so that all references to such a variable by the same name (even from functions compiled separately) are references to the same thing. In this sense, external variables are analogous to Fortran COMMON or PL/I EXTERNAL. We will see later how to define external variables and functions that are not globally available, but are instead visible only within a single source file.

Because external variables are globally accessible, they provide an alternative to function arguments and returned values for communicating data between functions. Any function may access an external variable by referring to it by name, if the name has been declared somehow.

If a large number of variables must be shared among functions, external variables are more convenient and efficient than long argument lists. As pointed out in Chapter 1, however, this reasoning should be applied with some caution, for it can have a bad effect on program structure, and lead to programs with many data connections between functions.

A second reason for using external variables concerns initialization. In particular, external arrays may be initialized, but automatic arrays may not. We will treat initialization near the end of this chapter.

The third reason for using external variables is their scope and lifetime. Automatic variables are internal to a function; they come into existence when the routine is entered, and disappear when it is left. External variables, on the other hand, are permanent. They do not come and go, so they retain values from one function invocation to the next. Thus if two functions must share some data, yet neither calls the other, it is often most convenient if the shared data is kept in external variables rather than passed in and out via arguments.

Let us examine this issue further with a larger example. The problem is to write another calculator program, better than the previous one. This one permits +, −, *, /, and = (to print the answer). Because it is somewhat easier to implement, the calculator will use reverse Polish notation instead of infix. (Reverse Polish is the scheme used by, for example, Hewlett-Packard pocket calculators.) In reverse Polish notation, each operator follows its operands; an infix expression like

```
(1 - 2) * (4 + 5) =
```

is entered as

```
1 2 - 4 5 + * =
```

Parentheses are not needed.

The implementation is quite simple. Each operand is pushed onto a stack; when an operator arrives, the proper number of operands (two for binary operators) are popped, the operator applied to them, and the result pushed back onto the stack. In the example above, for instance, 1 and 2 are pushed, then replaced by their difference, -1. Next, 4 and 5 are pushed and then replaced by their sum, 9. The product of -1 and 9, which is -9, replaces them on the stack. The = operator prints the top element without removing it (so intermediate steps in a calculation can be checked).

The operations of pushing and popping a stack are trivial, but by the time error detection and recovery are added, they are long enough that it is better to put each in a separate function than to repeat the code throughout the whole program. And there should be a separate function for fetching the next input operator or operand. Thus the structure of the program is

```
while (next operator or operand is not end of file)
      if (number)
            push it
      else if (operator)
            pop operands
            do operation
            push result
      else
            error
```

The main design decision that has not yet been discussed is where the stack is, that is, what routines access it directly. One possibility is to keep it in main, and pass the stack and the current stack position to the routines that push and pop it. But main doesn't need to know about the variables that control the stack; it should think only in terms of pushing and popping. So we have decided to make the stack and its associated information external variables accessible to the push and pop functions but not to main.

Translating this outline into code is easy enough. The main program is primarily a big switch on the type of operator or operand; this is perhaps a more typical use of switch than the one shown in Chapter 3.

```
#define MAXOP    20    /* max size of operand, operator */
#define NUMBER   '0'   /* signal that number found */
#define TOOBIG   '9'   /* signal that string is too big */

main()    /* reverse Polish desk calculator */
{
    int  type;
    char s[MAXOP];
    double op2, atof(), pop(), push();

    while ((type = getop(s, MAXOP)) != EOF)
        switch (type) {

        case NUMBER:
            push(atof(s));
            break;
        case '+':
            push(pop() + pop());
            break;
        case '*':
            push(pop() * pop());
            break;
        case '-':
            op2 = pop();
            push(pop() - op2);
            break;
        case '/':
            op2 = pop();
            if (op2 != 0.0)
                push(pop() / op2);
            else
                printf("zero divisor popped\n");
            break;
        case '=':
            printf("\t%f\n", push(pop()));
            break;
        case 'c':
            clear();
            break;
        case TOOBIG:
            printf("%.20s ... is too long\n", s);
            break;
        default:
            printf("unknown command %c\n", type);
            break;
        }
}
```

```
#define MAXVAL   100   /* maximum depth of val stack */

int sp = 0;     /* stack pointer */
double val[MAXVAL]; /* value stack */

double push(f) /* push f onto value stack */
double f;
{
    if (sp < MAXVAL)
        return(val[sp++] = f);
    else {
        printf("error: stack full\n");
        clear();
        return(0);
    }
}

double pop()    /* pop top value from stack */
{
    if (sp > 0)
        return(val[--sp]);
    else {
        printf("error: stack empty\n");
        clear();
        return(0);
    }
}

clear()    /* clear stack */
{
    sp = 0;
}
```

The command c clears the stack, with a function clear which is also used by push and pop in case of error. We'll return to getop in a moment.

As discussed in Chapter 1, a variable is external if it is defined outside the body of any function. Thus the stack and stack pointer which must be shared by push, pop, and clear are defined outside of these three functions. But main itself does *not* refer to the stack or stack pointer — the representation is carefully hidden. Thus the code for the = operator must use

```
push(pop());
```

to examine the top of the stack without disturbing it.

Notice also that because + and * are commutative operators, the order in which the popped operands are combined is irrelevant, but for the − and / operators, the left and right operands must be distinguished.

Exercise 4-3. Given the basic framework, it's straightforward to extend the calculator. Add the modulus (%) and unary minus operators. Add an "erase" command which erases the top entry on the stack. Add commands for handling variables. (Twenty-six single-letter variable names is easy.) □

4.5 Scope Rules

The functions and external variables that make up a C program need not all be compiled at the same time; the source text of the program may be kept in several files, and previously compiled routines may be loaded from libraries. The two questions of interest are

How are declarations written so that variables are properly declared during compilation?
How are declarations set up so that all the pieces will be properly connected when the program is loaded?

The *scope* of a name is the part of the program over which the name is defined. For an automatic variable declared at the beginning of a function, the scope is the function in which the name is declared, and variables of the same name in different functions are unrelated. The same is true of the arguments of the function.

The scope of an external variable lasts from the point at which it is declared in a source file to the end of that file. For example, if val, sp, push, pop, and clear are defined in one file, in the order shown above, that is,

```
int sp = 0;
double val[MAXVAL];

double push(f) { ... }

double pop() { ... }

clear() { ... }
```

then the variables val and sp may be used in push, pop and clear simply by naming them; no further declarations are needed.

On the other hand, if an external variable is to be referred to before it is defined, or if it is defined in a *different* source file from the one where it is being used, then an extern declaration is mandatory.

It is important to distinguish between the *declaration* of an external variable and its *definition*. A declaration announces the properties of a variable (its type, size, etc.); a definition also causes storage to be allocated. If the lines

```
int sp;
double val[MAXVAL];
```

appear outside of any function, they *define* the external variables `sp` and `val`, cause storage to be allocated, and also serve as the declaration for the rest of that source file. On the other hand, the lines

```
extern int sp;
extern double val[];
```

declare for the rest of the source file that `sp` is an `int` and that `val` is a `double` array (whose size is determined elsewhere), but they do not create the variables or allocate storage for them.

There must be only one *definition* of an external variable among all the files that make up the source program; other files may contain `extern` declarations to access it. (There may also be an `extern` declaration in the file containing the definition.) Any initialization of an external variable goes only with the definition. Array sizes must be specified with the definition, but are optional with an `extern` declaration.

Although it is not a likely organization for this program, `val` and `sp` could be defined and initialized in one file, and the functions `push`, `pop` and `clear` defined in another. Then these definitions and declarations would be necessary to tie them together:

In file 1:

```
int sp = 0;     /* stack pointer */
double val[MAXVAL]; /* value stack */
```

In file 2:

```
extern int sp;
extern double val[];

double push(f) { ... }

double pop() { ... }

clear() { ... }
```

Because the `extern` declarations in *file 2* lie ahead of and outside the three functions, they apply to all; one set of declarations suffices for all of *file 2.*

For larger programs, the `#include` file inclusion facility discussed later in this chapter allows one to keep only a single copy of the `extern` declarations for the program and have that inserted in each source file as it is being compiled.

Let us now turn to the implementation of `getop`, the function that fetches the next operator or operand. The basic task is easy: skip blanks, tabs and newlines. If the next character is not a digit or a decimal point, return it. Otherwise, collect a string of digits (that might include a decimal point), and return NUMBER, the signal that a number has been collected.

The routine is substantially complicated by an attempt to handle the situation properly when an input number is too long. getop reads digits (perhaps with an intervening decimal point) until it doesn't see any more, but only stores the ones that fit. If there was no overflow, it returns NUMBER and the string of digits. If the number was too long, however, getop discards the rest of the input line so the user can simply retype the line from the point of error; it returns TOOBIG as the overflow signal.

```
getop(s, lim)   /* get next operator or operand */
char s[];
int lim;
{
    int i, c;

    while ((c = getch()) == ' ' || c == '\t' || c == '\n')
        ;
    if (c != '.' && (c < '0' || c > '9'))
        return(c);
    s[0] = c;
    for (i = 1; (c = getchar()) >= '0' && c <= '9'; i++)
        if (i < lim)
            s[i] = c;
    if (c == '.') {       /* collect fraction */
        if (i < lim)
            s[i] = c;
        for (i++; (c=getchar()) >= '0' && c <= '9'; i++)
            if (i < lim)
                s[i] = c;
    }
    if (i < lim) { /* number is ok */
        ungetch(c);
        s[i] = '\0';
        return(NUMBER);
    } else {   /* it's too big; skip rest of line */
        while (c != '\n' && c != EOF)
            c = getchar();
        s[lim-1] = '\0';
        return(TOOBIG);
    }
}
```

What are getch and ungetch? It is often the case that a program reading input cannot determine that it has read enough until it has read too much. One instance is collecting the characters that make up a number:

until the first non-digit is seen, the number is not complete. But then the program has read one character too far, a character that it is not prepared for.

The problem would be solved if it were possible to "un-read" the unwanted character. Then, every time the program reads one character too many, it could push it back on the input, so the rest of the code could behave as if it had never been read. Fortunately, it's easy to simulate un-getting a character, by writing a pair of cooperating functions. getch delivers the next input character to be considered; ungetch puts a character back on the input, so that the next call to getch will return it again.

How they work together is simple. ungetch puts the pushed-back characters into a shared buffer — a character array. getch reads from the buffer if there is anything there; it calls getchar if the buffer is empty. There must also be an index variable which records the position of the current character in the buffer.

Since the buffer and the index are shared by getch and ungetch and must retain their values between calls, they must be external to both routines. Thus we can write getch, ungetch, and their shared variables as:

```
#define   BUFSIZE   100

char buf[BUFSIZE];   /* buffer for ungetch */
int  bufp = 0; /* next free position in buf */

getch()    /* get a (possibly pushed back) character */
{
    return((bufp > 0) ? buf[--bufp] : getchar());
}

ungetch(c)     /* push character back on input */
int c;
{
    if (bufp > BUFSIZE)
        printf("ungetch: too many characters\n");
    else
        buf[bufp++] = c;
}
```

We have used an array for the pushback, rather than a single character, since the generality may come in handy later.

Exercise 4-4. Write a routine ungets(s) which will push back an entire string onto the input. Should ungets know about buf and bufp, or should it just use ungetch? □

Exercise 4-5. Suppose that there will never be more than one character of pushback. Modify getch and ungetch accordingly. □

Exercise 4-6. Our `getch` and `ungetch` do not handle a pushed-back `EOF` in a portable way. Decide what their properties ought to be if an `EOF` is pushed back, then implement your design. □

4.6   Static Variables

Static variables are a third class of storage, in addition to the `extern` and automatic that we have already met.

`static` variables may be either internal or external. Internal `static` variables are local to a particular function just as automatic variables are, but unlike automatics, they remain in existence rather than coming and going each time the function is activated. This means that internal `static` variables provide private, permanent storage in a function. Character strings that appear within a function, such as the arguments of `printf`, are internal static.

An external `static` variable is known within the remainder of the *source file* in which it is declared, but not in any other file. External `static` thus provides a way to hide names like `buf` and `bufp` in the `getch`–`ungetch` combination, which must be external so they can be shared, yet which should not be visible to users of `getch` and `ungetch`, so there is no possibility of conflict. If the two routines and the two variables are compiled in one file, as

```
static char    buf[BUFSIZE];   /* buffer for ungetch */
static int     bufp = 0; /* next free position in buf */

getch() { ... }

ungetch(c) { ... }
```

then no other routine will be able to access `buf` and `bufp`; in fact, they will not conflict with the same names in other files of the same program.

Static storage, whether internal or external, is specified by prefixing the normal declaration with the word `static`. The variable is external if it is defined outside of any function, and internal if defined inside a function.

Normally, functions are external objects; their names are known globally. It is possible, however, for a function to be declared `static`; this makes its name unknown outside of the file in which it is declared.

In C, "`static`" connotes not only permanence but also a degree of what might be called "privacy." Internal `static` objects are known only inside one function; external `static` objects (variables or functions) are known only within the source file in which they appear, and their names do not interfere with variables or functions of the same name in other files.

External `static` variables and functions provide a way to conceal data objects and any internal routines that manipulate them so that other routines and data cannot conflict even inadvertently. For example, `getch` and `ungetch` form a "module" for character input and pushback; `buf` and `bufp` should be `static` so they are inaccessible from the outside. In the same way, `push`, `pop` and `clear` form a module for stack manipulation; `val` and `sp` should also be external `static`.

4.7 Register Variables

The fourth and final storage class is called `register`. A `register` declaration advises the compiler that the variable in question will be heavily used. When possible, `register` variables are placed in machine registers, which may result in smaller and faster programs.

The `register` declaration looks like

```
register int   x;
register char  c;
```

and so on; the `int` part may be omitted. `register` can only be applied to automatic variables and to the formal parameters of a function. In this latter case, the declaration looks like

```
f(c, n)
register int c, n;
{
        register int i;
        ...
}
```

In practice, there are some restrictions on register variables, reflecting the realities of underlying hardware. Only a few variables in each function may be kept in registers, and only certain types are allowed. The word `register` is ignored for excess or disallowed declarations. And it is not possible to take the address of a register variable (a topic to be covered in Chapter 5). The specific restrictions vary from machine to machine; as an example, on the PDP-11, only the first three register declarations in a function are effective, and the types must be `int`, `char`, or pointer.

4.8 Block Structure

C is not a block-structured language in the sense of PL/I or Algol, in that functions may not be defined within other functions.

On the other hand, variables can be defined in a block-structured fashion. Declarations of variables (including initializations) may follow the left brace that introduces *any* compound statement, not just the one that begins a function. Variables declared in this way supersede any identically named variables in outer blocks, and remain in existence until the matching right brace. For example, in

```
if (n > 0) {
    int i;      /* declare a new i */
    for (i = 0; i < n; i++)
        ...
}
```

the scope of the variable i is the "true" branch of the if; this i is unrelated to any other i in the program.

Block structure also applies to external variables. Given the declarations

```
int x;

f()
{
    double x;
    ...
}
```

then within the function f, occurrences of x refer to the internal double variable; outside of f, they refer to the external integer. The same is true of the names of formal parameters:

```
int z;

f(z)
double z;
{
    ...
}
```

Within the function f, z refers to the formal parameter, not the external.

4.9   Initialization

Initialization has been mentioned in passing many times so far, but always peripherally to some other topic. This section summarizes some of the rules, now that we have discussed the various storage classes.

In the absence of explicit initialization, external and static variables are guaranteed to be initialized to zero; automatic and register variables have undefined (i.e., garbage) values.

Simple variables (not arrays or structures) may be initialized when they are declared, by following the name with an equals sign and a constant expression:

```
int   x = 1;
char squote = '\'';
long day = 60 * 24; /* minutes in a day */
```

For external and static variables, the initialization is done once, conceptually at compile time. For automatic and register variables, it is done each time the function or block is entered.

For automatic and register variables, the initializer is not restricted to being a constant: it may in fact be any valid expression involving previously defined values, even function calls. For example, the initializations of the binary search program in Chapter 3 could be written as

```
binary(x, v, n)
int x, v[], n;
{
      int low = 0;
      int high = n - 1;
      int mid;
      ...
}
```

instead of

```
binary(x, v, n)
int x, v[], n;
{
      int low, high, mid;

      low = 0;
      high = n - 1;
      ...
}
```

In effect, initializations of automatic variables are just shorthand for assignment statements. Which form to prefer is largely a matter of taste. We have generally used explicit assignments, because initializers in declarations are harder to see.

Automatic arrays may not be initialized. External and static arrays may be initialized by following the declaration with a list of initializers enclosed in braces and separated by commas. For example, the character counting program of Chapter 1, which began

```
main()    /* count digits, white space, others */
{
      int c, i, nwhite, nother;
      int ndigit[10];

      nwhite = nother = 0;
      for (i = 0; i < 10; i++)
            ndigit[i] = 0;
      ...
}
```

can be written instead as

```
int   nwhite = 0;
int   nother = 0;
int   ndigit[10] ={ 0, 0, 0, 0, 0, 0, 0, 0, 0, 0 };

main()      /* count digits, white space, others */
{
     int c, i;
     ...
}
```

These initializations are actually unnecessary since all are zero, but it's good form to make them explicit anyway. If there are fewer initializers than the specified size, the others will be zero. It is an error to have too many initializers. Regrettably, there is no way to specify repetition of an initializer, nor to initialize an element in the middle of an array without supplying all the intervening values as well.

Character arrays are a special case of initialization; a string may be used instead of the braces and commas notation:

```
char pattern[] = "the";
```

This is a shorthand for the longer but equivalent

```
char pattern[] = { 't', 'h', 'e', '\0' };
```

When the size of an array of any type is omitted, the compiler will compute the length by counting the initializers. In this specific case, the size is 4 (three characters plus the terminating \0).

4.10 Recursion

C functions may be used recursively; that is, a function may call *itself* either directly or indirectly. One traditional example involves printing a number as a character string. As we mentioned before, the digits are generated in the wrong order: low-order digits are available before high-order digits, but they have to be printed the other way around.

There are two solutions to this problem. One is to store the digits in an array as they are generated, then print them in the reverse order, as we did in Chapter 3 with itoa. The first version of printd follows this pattern.

```
printd(n) /* print n in decimal */
int n;
{
     char s[10];
     int i;

     if (n < 0) {
         putchar('-');
         n = -n;
     }
     i = 0;
     do {
         s[i++] = n % 10 + '0';    /* get next char */
     } while ((n /= 10) > 0); /* discard it */
     while (--i >= 0)
         putchar(s[i]);
}
```

The alternative is a recursive solution, in which each call of `printd` first calls itself to cope with any leading digits, then prints the trailing digit.

```
printd(n) /* print n in decimal (recursive) */
int n;
{
     int i;

     if (n < 0) {
         putchar('-');
         n = -n;
     }
     if ((i = n/10) != 0)
         printd(i);
     putchar(n % 10 + '0');
}
```

When a function calls itself recursively, each invocation gets a fresh set of all the automatic variables, quite independent of the previous set. Thus in `printd(123)` the first `printd` has n = 123. It passes 12 to a second `printd`, then prints 3 when that one returns. In the same way, the second `printd` passes 1 to a third (which prints it), then prints 2.

Recursion generally provides no saving in storage, since somewhere a stack of the values being processed has to be maintained. Nor will it be faster. But recursive code is more compact, and often much easier to write and understand. Recursion is especially convenient for recursively defined data structures like trees; we will see a nice example in Chapter 6.

Exercise 4-7. Adapt the ideas of `printd` to write a recursive version of `itoa`; that is, convert an integer into a string with a recursive routine. □

Exercise 4-8. Write a recursive version of the function `reverse(s)`, which reverses the string `s`. □

4.11   The C Preprocessor

C provides certain language extensions by means of a simple macro preprocessor. The `#define` capability which we have used is the most common of these extensions; another is the ability to include the contents of other files during compilation.

File Inclusion

To facilitate handling collections of `#define`'s and declarations (among other things) C provides a file inclusion feature. Any line that looks like

```
#include "filename"
```

is replaced by the contents of the file *filename*. (The quotes are mandatory.) Often a line or two of this form appears at the beginning of each source file, to include common `#define` statements and `extern` declarations for global variables. `#include`'s may be nested.

`#include` is the preferred way to tie the declarations together for a large program. It guarantees that all the source files will be supplied with the same definitions and variable declarations, and thus eliminates a particularly nasty kind of bug. Of course, when an included file is changed, all files that depend on it must be recompiled.

Macro Substitution

A definition of the form

```
#define   YES   1
```

calls for a macro substitution of the simplest kind — replacing a name by a string of characters. Names in `#define` have the same form as C identifiers; the replacement text is arbitrary. Normally the replacement text is the rest of the line; a long definition may be continued by placing a \ at the end of the line to be continued. The "scope" of a name defined with `#define` is from its point of definition to the end of the source file. Names may be redefined, and a definition may use previous definitions. Substitutions do not take place within quoted strings, so, for example, if `YES` is a defined name, there would be no substitution in `printf("YES")`.

Since implementation of `#define` is a macro prepass, not part of the compiler proper, there are very few grammatical restrictions on what can be defined. For example, Algol fans can say

```
#define then
#define begin   {
#define end     ; }
```

and then write

```
if (i > 0) then
    begin
         a = 1;
         b = 2
    end
```

It is also possible to define macros with arguments, so the replacement text depends on the way the macro is called. As an example, define a macro called `max` like this:

```
#define  max(A, B)   ((A) > (B) ? (A) : (B))
```

Now the line

```
x = max(p+q, r+s);
```

will be replaced by the line

```
x = ((p+q) > (r+s) ? (p+q) : (r+s));
```

This provides a "maximum function" that expands into in-line code rather than a function call. So long as the arguments are treated consistently, this macro will serve for any data type; there is no need for different kinds of `max` for different data types, as there would be with functions.

Of course, if you examine the expansion of `max` above, you will notice some pitfalls. The expressions are evaluated twice; this is bad if they involve side effects like function calls and increment operators. Some care has to be taken with parentheses to make sure the order of evaluation is preserved. (Consider the macro

```
#define  square(x)  x * x
```

when invoked as `square(z+1)`.) There are even some purely lexical problems: there can be no space between the macro name and the left parenthesis that introduces its argument list.

Nonetheless, macros are quite valuable. One practical example is the standard I/O library to be described in Chapter 7, in which `getchar` and `putchar` are defined as macros (obviously `putchar` needs an argument), thus avoiding the overhead of a function call per character processed.

Other capabilities of the macro processor are described in Appendix A.

Exercise 4-9. Define a macro `swap(x, y)` which interchanges its two `int` arguments. (Block structure will help.) □

CHAPTER 5: POINTERS AND ARRAYS

A pointer is a variable that contains the address of another variable. Pointers are very much used in C, partly because they are sometimes the only way to express a computation, and partly because they usually lead to more compact and efficient code than can be obtained in other ways.

Pointers have been lumped with the `goto` statement as a marvelous way to create impossible-to-understand programs. This is certainly true when they are used carelessly, and it is easy to create pointers that point somewhere unexpected. With discipline, however, pointers can also be used to achieve clarity and simplicity. This is the aspect that we will try to illustrate.

5.1 Pointers and Addresses

Since a pointer contains the address of an object, it is possible to access the object "indirectly" through the pointer. Suppose that **x** is a variable, say an `int`, and that **px** is a pointer, created in some as yet unspecified way. The unary operator **&** gives the *address* of an object, so the statement

```
px = &x;
```

assigns the address of **x** to the variable **px**; **px** is now said to "point to" **x**. The **&** operator can be applied only to variables and array elements; constructs like **&(x+1)** and **&3** are illegal. It is also illegal to take the address of a `register` variable.

The unary operator ***** treats its operand as the address of the ultimate target, and accesses that address to fetch the contents. Thus if **y** is also an `int`,

```
y = *px;
```

assigns to **y** the contents of whatever **px** points to. So the sequence

```
px = &x;
y = *px;
```

assigns the same value to **y** as does

89

```
y = x;
```

It is also necessary to declare the variables that participate in all of this:

```
int   x, y;
int   *px;
```

The declaration of x and y is what we've seen all along. The declaration of the pointer px is new.

```
int   *px;
```

is intended as a mnemonic; it says that the combination *px is an int, that is, if px occurs in the context *px, it is equivalent to a variable of type int. In effect, the syntax of the declaration for a variable mimics the syntax of expressions in which the variable might appear. This reasoning is useful in all cases involving complicated declarations. For example,

```
double atof(), *dp;
```

says that in an expression atof() and *dp have values of type double.

You should also note the implication in the declaration that a pointer is constrained to point to a particular kind of object.

Pointers can occur in expressions. For example, if px points to the integer x, then *px can occur in any context where x could.

```
y = *px + 1
```

sets y to 1 more than x;

```
printf("%d\n", *px)
```

prints the current value of x; and

```
d = sqrt((double) *px)
```

produces in d the square root of x, which is coerced into a double before being passed to sqrt. (See Chapter 2.)

In expressions like

```
y = *px + 1
```

the unary operators * and & bind more tightly than arithmetic operators, so this expression takes whatever px points at, adds 1, and assigns it to y. We will return shortly to what

```
y = *(px + 1)
```

might mean.

Pointer references can also occur on the left side of assignments. If px points to x, then

```
*px = 0
```

sets **x** to zero, and

```
*px += 1
```

increments it, as does

```
(*px)++
```

The parentheses are necessary in this last example; without them, the expression would increment **px** instead of what it points to, because unary operators like ***** and **++** are evaluated right to left.

Finally, since pointers are variables, they can be manipulated as other variables can. If **py** is another pointer to **int**, then

```
py = px
```

copies the contents of **px** into **py**, thus making **py** point to whatever **px** points to.

5.2   Pointers and Function Arguments

Since C passes arguments to functions by "call by value," there is no direct way for the called function to alter a variable in the calling function. What do you do if you really have to change an ordinary argument? For example, a sorting routine might exchange two out-of-order elements with a function called **swap**. It is not enough to write

```
swap(a, b);
```

where the **swap** function is defined as

```
swap(x, y)      /* WRONG */
int x, y;
{
    int temp;

    temp = x;
    x = y;
    y = temp;
}
```

Because of call by value, **swap** *can't* affect the arguments **a** and **b** in the routine that called it.

Fortunately, there is a way to obtain the desired effect. The calling program passes *pointers* to the values to be changed:

```
swap(&a, &b);
```

Since the operator **&** gives the address of a variable, **&a** is a pointer to **a**. In **swap** itself, the arguments are declared to be pointers, and the actual operands are accessed through them.

```
swap(px, py)    /* interchange *px and *py */
int *px, *py;
{
        int temp;

        temp = *px;
        *px = *py;
        *py = temp;
}
```

One common use of pointer arguments is in functions that must return more than a single value. (You might say that swap returns two values, the new values of its arguments.) As an example, consider a function getint which performs free-format input conversion by breaking a stream of characters into integer values, one integer per call. getint has to return the value it found, or an end of file signal when there is no more input. These values have to be returned as separate objects, for no matter what value is used for EOF, that could also be the value of an input integer.

One solution, which is based on the input function scanf that we will describe in Chapter 7, is to have getint return EOF as its function value if it found end of file; any other returned value signals a normal integer. The numeric value of the integer it found is returned through an argument, which must be a pointer to an integer. This organization separates end of file status from numeric values.

The following loop fills an array with integers by calls to getint:

```
int n, v, array[SIZE];

for (n = 0; n < SIZE && getint(&v) != EOF; n++)
        array[n] = v;
```

Each call sets v to the next integer found in the input. Notice that it is essential to write &v instead of v as the argument of getint. Using plain v is likely to cause an addressing error, since getint believes it has been handed a valid pointer.

getint itself is an obvious modification of the atoi we wrote earlier:

```
getint(pn)        /* get next integer from input */
int *pn;
{
    int c, sign;

    while ((c = getch()) == ' ' || c == '\n' || c == '\t')
        ;      /* skip white space */
    sign = 1;
    if (c == '+' || c == '-') {    /* record sign */
        sign = (c=='+') ? 1 : -1;
        c = getch();
    }
    for (*pn = 0; c >= '0' && c <= '9'; c = getch())
        *pn = 10 * *pn + c - '0';
    *pn *= sign;
    if (c != EOF)
        ungetch(c);
    return(c);
}
```

Throughout `getint`, `*pn` is used as an ordinary `int` variable. We have also used `getch` and `ungetch` (described in Chapter 4) so the one extra character that must be read can be pushed back onto the input.

Exercise 5-1. Write `getfloat`, the floating point analog of `getint`. What type does `getfloat` return as its function value? □

5.3 Pointers and Arrays

In C, there is a strong relationship between pointers and arrays, strong enough that pointers and arrays really should be treated simultaneously. Any operation which can be achieved by array subscripting can also be done with pointers. The pointer version will in general be faster but, at least to the uninitiated, somewhat harder to grasp immediately.

The declaration

```
int a[10]
```

defines an array `a` of size 10, that is a block of 10 consecutive objects named `a[0]`, `a[1]`, ..., `a[9]`. The notation `a[i]` means the element of the array `i` positions from the beginning. If `pa` is a pointer to an integer, declared as

```
int *pa
```

then the assignment

```
pa = &a[0]
```

sets `pa` to point to the zeroth element of `a`; that is, `pa` contains the address of a[0]. Now the assignment

```
x = *pa
```

will copy the contents of a[0] into **x**.

If pa points to a particular element of an array a, then *by definition* pa+1 points to the next element, and in general pa−i points i elements before pa, and pa+i points i elements after. Thus, if pa points to a[0],

```
*(pa+1)
```

refers to the contents of a[1], pa+i is the address of a[i], and *(pa+i) is the contents of a[i].

These remarks are true regardless of the type of the variables in the array a. The definition of "adding 1 to a pointer," and by extension, all pointer arithmetic, is that the increment is scaled by the size in storage of the object that is pointed to. Thus in pa+i, i is multiplied by the size of the objects that pa points to before being added to pa.

The correspondence between indexing and pointer arithmetic is evidently very close. In fact, a reference to an array is converted by the compiler to a pointer to the beginning of the array. The effect is that an array name *is* a pointer expression. This has quite a few useful implications. Since the name of an array is a synonym for the location of the zeroth element, the assignment

```
pa = &a[0]
```

can also be written as

```
pa = a
```

Rather more surprising, at least at first sight, is the fact that a reference to a[i] can also be written as *(a+i). In evaluating a[i], C converts it to *(a+i) immediately; the two forms are completely equivalent. Applying the operator & to both parts of this equivalence, it follows that &a[i] and a+i are also identical: a+i is the address of the i-th element beyond a. As the other side of this coin, if pa is a pointer, expressions may use it with a subscript: pa[i] is identical to *(pa+i). In short, any array and index expression can be written as a pointer and offset, and vice versa, even in the same statement.

There is one difference between an array name and a pointer that must be kept in mind. A pointer is a variable, so pa=a and pa++ are sensible operations. But an array name is a *constant*, not a variable: constructions like a=pa or a++ or p=&a are illegal.

When an array name is passed to a function, what is passed is the location of the beginning of the array. Within the called function, this argument is a variable, just like any other variable, and so an array name argument is truly a pointer, that is, a variable containing an address. We can use this fact to write a new version of `strlen`, which computes the length of a string.

```
strlen(s) /* return length of string s */
char *s;
{
    int n;

    for (n = 0; *s != '\0'; s++)
        n++;
    return(n);
}
```

Incrementing `s` is perfectly legal, since it is a pointer variable; `s++` has no effect on the character string in the function that called `strlen`, but merely increments `strlen`'s private copy of the address.

As formal parameters in a function definition,

```
char s[];
```

and

```
char *s;
```

are exactly equivalent; which one should be written is determined largely by how expressions will be written in the function. When an array name is passed to a function, the function can at its convenience believe that it has been handed either an array or a pointer, and manipulate it accordingly. It can even use both kinds of operations if it seems appropriate and clear.

It is possible to pass part of an array to a function, by passing a pointer to the beginning of the subarray. For example, if `a` is an array,

```
f(&a[2])
```

and

```
f(a+2)
```

both pass to the function `f` the address of element `a[2]`, because `&a[2]` and `a+2` are both pointer expressions that refer to the third element of `a`. Within `f`, the argument declaration can read

```
f(arr)
int arr[];
{
    ...
}
```

or

```
f(arr)
int *arr;
{
    ...
}
```

So as far as f is concerned, the fact that the argument really refers to part of a larger array is of no consequence.

5.4   Address Arithmetic

If p is a pointer, then p++ increments p to point to the next element of whatever kind of object p points to, and p+=i increments p to point i elements beyond where it currently does. These and similar constructions are the simplest and most common forms of pointer or address arithmetic.

C is consistent and regular in its approach to address arithmetic; its integration of pointers, arrays and address arithmetic is one of the major strengths of the language. Let us illustrate some of its properties by writing a rudimentary storage allocator (but useful in spite of its simplicity). There are two routines: alloc(n) returns a pointer p to n consecutive character positions, which can be used by the caller of alloc for storing characters; free(p) releases the storage thus acquired so it can be later re-used. The routines are "rudimentary" because the calls to free must be made in the opposite order to the calls made on alloc. That is, the storage managed by alloc and free is a stack, or last-in, first-out list. The standard C library provides analogous functions which have no such restrictions, and in Chapter 8 we will show improved versions as well. In the meantime, however, many applications really only need a trivial alloc to dispense little pieces of storage of unpredictable sizes at unpredictable times.

The simplest implementation is to have alloc hand out pieces of a large character array which we will call allocbuf. This array is private to alloc and free. Since they deal in pointers, not array indices, no other routine need know the name of the array, which can be declared external static, that is, local to the source file containing alloc and free, and invisible outside it. In practical implementations, the array may well not even have a name; it might instead be obtained by asking the operating system for a pointer to some unnamed block of storage.

The other information needed is how much of allocbuf has been used. We use a pointer to the next free element, called allocp. When alloc is asked for n characters, it checks to see if there is enough room left in allocbuf. If so, alloc returns the current value of allocp (i.e., the beginning of the free block), then increments it by n to point to the next free area. free(p) merely sets allocp to p if p is inside allocbuf.

```
#define    NULL 0     /* pointer value for error report */
#define    ALLOCSIZE 1000 /* size of available space */

static char allocbuf[ALLOCSIZE];   /* storage for alloc */
static char *allocp = allocbuf;   /* next free position */

char *alloc(n) /* return pointer to n characters */
int n;
{
    if (allocp + n <= allocbuf + ALLOCSIZE) { /* fits */
        allocp += n;
        return(allocp - n); /* old p */
    } else          /* not enough room */
        return(NULL);
}

free(p)    /* free storage pointed to by p */
char *p;
{
    if (p >= allocbuf && p < allocbuf + ALLOCSIZE)
        allocp = p;
}
```

Some explanations. In general a pointer can be initialized just as any other variable can, though normally the only meaningful values are NULL (discussed below) or an expression involving addresses of previously defined data of appropriate type. The declaration

```
static char *allocp = allocbuf;
```

defines allocp to be a character pointer and initializes it to point to allocbuf, which is the next free position when the program starts. This could have also been written

```
static char *allocp = &allocbuf[0];
```

since the array name *is* the address of the zeroth element; use whichever is more natural.

The test

```
if (allocp + n <= allocbuf + ALLOCSIZE)
```

checks if there's enough room to satisfy a request for n characters. If there is, the new value of allocp would be at most one beyond the end of allocbuf. If the request can be satisfied, alloc returns a normal pointer (notice the declaration of the function itself). If not, alloc must return some signal that no space is left. C guarantees that no pointer that validly points at data will contain zero, so a return value of zero can be used to signal an abnormal event, in this case, no space. We write NULL instead of zero, however, to indicate more clearly that this is a special value for a pointer. In general, integers cannot meaningfully be assigned to pointers; zero is a special case.

Tests like

```
if (allocp + n <= allocbuf + ALLOCSIZE)
```

and

```
if (p >= allocbuf && p < allocbuf + ALLOCSIZE)
```

show several important facets of pointer arithmetic. First, pointers may be compared under certain circumstances. If p and q point to members of the same array, then relations like <, >=, etc., work properly.

```
p < q
```

is true, for example, if p points to an earlier member of the array than does q. The relations == and != also work. Any pointer can be meaningfully compared for equality or inequality with NULL. But all bets are off if you do arithmetic or comparisons with pointers pointing to different arrays. If you're lucky, you'll get obvious nonsense on all machines. If you're unlucky, your code will work on one machine but collapse mysteriously on another.

Second, we have already observed that a pointer and an integer may be added or subtracted. The construction

```
p + n
```

means the n-th object beyond the one p currently points to. This is true regardless of the kind of object p is declared to point at; the compiler scales n according to the size of the objects p points to, which is determined by the declaration of p. For example, on the PDP-11, the scale factors are 1 for char, 2 for int and short, 4 for long and float, and 8 for double.

Pointer subtraction is also valid: if p and q point to members of the same array, p-q is the number of elements between p and q. This fact can be used to write yet another version of strlen:

```
strlen(s) /* return length of string s */
char *s;
{
    char *p = s;

    while (*p != '\0')
        p++;
    return(p-s);
}
```

In its declaration, p is initialized to s, that is, to point to the first character.

In the `while` loop, each character in turn is examined until the `\0` at the end is seen. Since `\0` is zero, and since `while` tests only whether the expression is zero, it is possible to omit the explicit test, and such loops are often written as

```
while (*p)
      p++;
```

Because `p` points to characters, `p++` advances `p` to the next character each time, and `p-s` gives the number of characters advanced over, that is, the string length. Pointer arithmetic is consistent: if we had been dealing with `float`'s, which occupy more storage than `char`'s, and if `p` were a pointer to `float`, `p++` would advance to the next `float`. Thus we could write another version of `alloc` which maintains, let us say, `float`'s instead of `char`'s, merely by changing `char` to `float` throughout `alloc` and `free`. All the pointer manipulations automatically take into account the size of the object pointed to, so nothing else has to be altered.

Other than the operations mentioned here (adding or subtracting a pointer and an integer; subtracting or comparing two pointers), all other pointer arithmetic is illegal. It is not permitted to add two pointers, or to multiply or divide or shift or mask them, or to add `float` or `double` to them.

5.5   Character Pointers and Functions

A *string constant*, written as

```
"I am a string"
```

is an array of characters. In the internal representation, the compiler terminates the array with the character `\0` so that programs can find the end. The length in storage is thus one more than the number of characters between the double quotes.

Perhaps the most common occurrence of string constants is as arguments to functions, as in

```
printf("hello, world\n");
```

When a character string like this appears in a program, access to it is through a character pointer; what `printf` receives is a pointer to the character array.

Character arrays of course need not be function arguments. If `message` is declared as

```
char *message;
```

then the statement

```
message = "now is the time";
```

assigns to `message` a pointer to the actual characters. This is *not* a string copy; only pointers are involved. C does not provide any operators for processing an entire string of characters as a unit.

We will illustrate more aspects of pointers and arrays by studying two useful functions from the standard I/O library to be discussed in Chapter 7.

The first function is `strcpy(s, t)`, which copies the string `t` to the string `s`. The arguments are written in this order by analogy to assignment, where one would say

```
s = t
```

to assign `t` to `s`. The array version is first:

```
strcpy(s, t)    /* copy t to s */
char s[], t[];
{
      int i;

      i = 0;
      while ((s[i] = t[i]) != '\0')
            i++;
}
```

For contrast, here is a version of `strcpy` with pointers.

```
strcpy(s, t)    /* copy t to s; pointer version 1 */
char *s, *t;
{
      while ((*s = *t) != '\0') {
            s++;
            t++;
      }
}
```

Because arguments are passed by value, `strcpy` can use `s` and `t` in any way it pleases. Here they are conveniently initialized pointers, which are marched along the arrays a character at a time, until the \0 which terminates `t` has been copied to `s`.

In practice, `strcpy` would not be written as we showed it above. A second possibility might be

```
strcpy(s, t)    /* copy t to s; pointer version 2 */
char *s, *t;
{
      while ((*s++ = *t++) != '\0')
            ;
}
```

This moves the increment of s and t into the test part. The value of *t++ is the character that t pointed to before t was incremented; the postfix ++ doesn't change t until after this character has been fetched. In the same way, the character is stored into the old s position before s is incremented. This character is also the value that is compared against \0 to control the loop. The net effect is that characters are copied from t to s up to and including the terminating \0.

   As the final abbreviation, we again observe that a comparison against \0 is redundant, so the function is often written as

```
strcpy(s, t)    /* copy t to s; pointer version 3 */
char *s, *t;
{
      while (*s++ = *t++)
            ;
}
```

Although this may seem cryptic at first sight, the notational convenience is considerable, and the idiom should be mastered, if for no other reason than that you will see it frequently in C programs.

   The second routine is strcmp(s, t), which compares the character strings s and t, and returns negative, zero or positive according as s is lexicographically less than, equal to, or greater than t. The value returned is obtained by subtracting the characters at the first position where s and t disagree.

```
strcmp(s, t)   /* return <0 if s<t, 0 if s==t, >0 if s>t */
char s[], t[];
{
      int i;

      i = 0;
      while (s[i] == t[i])
            if (s[i++] == '\0')
                  return(0);
      return(s[i] - t[i]);
}
```

The pointer version of strcmp:

```
strcmp(s, t)   /* return <0 if s<t, 0 if s==t, >0 if s>t */
char *s, *t;
{
      for ( ; *s == *t; s++, t++)
            if (*s == '\0')
                  return(0);
      return(*s - *t);
}
```

Since ++ and -- are either prefix or postfix operators, other combinations of * and ++ and -- occur, although less frequently. For example,

```
*++p
```

increments p *before* fetching the character that p points to;

```
*--p
```

decrements p first.

Exercise 5-2. Write a pointer version of the function `strcat` which we showed in Chapter 2: `strcat(s, t)` copies the string t to the end of s. □

Exercise 5-3. Write a macro for `strcpy`. □

Exercise 5-4. Rewrite appropriate programs from earlier chapters and exercises with pointers instead of array indexing. Good possibilities include `getline` (Chapters 1 and 4), `atoi`, `itoa`, and their variants (Chapters 2, 3, and 4), `reverse` (Chapter 3), and `index` and `getop` (Chapter 4). □

5.6   Pointers are not Integers

You may notice in older C programs a rather cavalier attitude toward copying pointers. It has generally been true that on most machines a pointer may be assigned to an integer and back again without changing it; no scaling or conversion takes place, and no bits are lost. Regrettably, this has led to the taking of liberties with routines that return pointers which are then merely passed to other routines — the requisite pointer declarations are often left out. For example, consider the function `strsave(s)`, which copies the string s into a safe place, obtained by a call on `alloc`, and returns a pointer to it. Properly, this should be written as

```
        char *strsave(s)      /* save string s somewhere */
        char *s;
        {
                char *p, *alloc();

                if ((p = alloc(strlen(s)+1)) != NULL)
                        strcpy(p, s);
                return(p);
        }
```

In practice, there would be a strong tendency to omit declarations:

```
        strsave(s)            /* save string s somewhere */
        {
                char *p;

                if ((p = alloc(strlen(s)+1)) != NULL)
                        strcpy(p, s);
                return(p);
        }
```

This will work on many machines, since the default type for functions and
arguments is int, and int and pointer can usually be safely assigned back
and forth. Nevertheless this kind of code is inherently risky, for it depends
on details of implementation and machine architecture which may not hold
for the particular compiler you use. It's wiser to be complete in all declarations. (The program *lint* will warn of such constructions, in case they creep
in inadvertently.)

5.7 Multi-Dimensional Arrays

C provides for rectangular multi-dimensional arrays, although in practice
they tend to be much less used than arrays of pointers. In this section, we
will show some of their properties.

Consider the problem of date conversion, from day of the month to day
of the year and vice versa. For example, March 1 is the 60th day of a non-
leap year, and the 61st day of a leap year. Let us define two functions to do
the conversions: day_of_year converts the month and day into the day of
the year, and month_day converts the day of the year into the month and
day. Since this latter function returns two values, the month and day arguments will be pointers:

```
        month_day(1977, 60, &m, &d)
```

sets m to 3 and d to 1 (March 1st).

These functions both need the same information, a table of the number
of days in each month ("thirty days hath September ..."). Since the
number of days per month differs for leap years and non-leap years, it's

easier to separate them into two rows of a two-dimensional array than try to keep track of what happens to February during computation. The array and the functions for performing the transformations are as follows:

```
static int day_tab[2][13] ={
       {0, 31, 28, 31, 30, 31, 30, 31, 31, 30, 31, 30, 31},
       {0, 31, 29, 31, 30, 31, 30, 31, 31, 30, 31, 30, 31}
};

day_of_year(year, month, day) /* set day of year */
int year, month, day;         /* from month & day */
{
       int i, leap;

       leap = year%4 == 0 && year%100 != 0 || year%400 == 0;
       for (i = 1; i < month; i++)
             day += day_tab[leap][i];
       return(day);
}

month_day(year, yearday, pmonth, pday) /* set month, day */
int year, yearday, *pmonth, *pday; /* from day of year */
{
       int i, leap;

       leap = year%4 == 0 && year%100 != 0 || year%400 == 0;
       for (i = 1; yearday > day_tab[leap][i]; i++)
             yearday -= day_tab[leap][i];
       *pmonth = i;
       *pday = yearday;
}
```

The array `day_tab` has to be external to both `day_of_year` and `month_day`, so they can both use it.

`day_tab` is the first two-dimensional array we have dealt with. In C, by definition a two-dimensional array is really a one-dimensional array, each of whose elements is an array. Hence subscripts are written as

```
day_tab[i][j]
```

rather than

```
day_tab[i, j]
```

as in most languages. Other than this, a two-dimensional array can be treated in much the same way as in other languages. Elements are stored by rows, that is, the rightmost subscript varies fastest as elements are accessed in storage order.

An array is initialized by a list of initializers in braces; each row of a two-dimensional array is initialized by a corresponding sub-list. We started the array `day_tab` with a column of zero so that month numbers can run from the natural 1 to 12 instead of 0 to 11. Since space is not at a premium here, this is easier than adjusting indices.

If a two-dimensional array is to be passed to a function, the argument declaration in the function *must* include the column dimension; the row dimension is irrelevant, since what is passed is, as before, a pointer. In this particular case, it is a pointer to objects which are arrays of 13 `int`'s. Thus if the array `day_tab` is to be passed to a function `f`, the declaration of `f` would be

```
f(day_tab)
int day_tab[2] [13];
{
       ...
}
```

The argument declaration in `f` could also be

```
int day_tab[] [13];
```

since the number of rows is irrelevant, or it could be

```
int (*day_tab) [13];
```

which says that the argument is a pointer to an array of 13 integers. The parentheses are necessary since brackets `[]` have higher precedence than `*`; without parentheses, the declaration

```
int *day_tab[13];
```

is an array of 13 pointers to integers, as we shall see in the next section.

5.8 Pointer Arrays; Pointers to Pointers

Since pointers are variables themselves, you might expect that there would be uses for arrays of pointers. This is indeed the case. Let us illustrate by writing a program that will sort a set of text lines into alphabetic order, a stripped-down version of the UNIX utility *sort*.

In Chapter 3 we presented a Shell sort function that would sort an array of integers. The same algorithm will work, except that now we have to deal with lines of text, which are of different lengths, and which, unlike integers, can't be compared or moved in a single operation. We need a data representation that will cope efficiently and conveniently with variable-length text lines.

This is where the array of pointers enters. If the lines to be sorted are stored end-to-end in one long character array (maintained by `alloc`, perhaps), then each line can be accessed by a pointer to its first character.

The pointers themselves can be stored in an array. Two lines can be compared by passing their pointers to strcmp. When two out-of-order lines have to be exchanged, the *pointers* in the pointer array are exchanged, not the text lines themselves. This eliminates the twin problems of complicated storage management and high overhead that would go with moving the actual lines.

The sorting process involves three steps:

> *read all the lines of input*
> *sort them*
> *print them in order*

As usual, it's best to divide the program into functions that match this natural division, with the main routine controlling things.

Let us defer the sorting step for a moment, and concentrate on the data structure and the input and output. The input routine has to collect and save the characters of each line, and build an array of pointers to the lines. It will also have to count the number of input lines, since that information is needed for sorting and printing. Since the input function can only cope with a finite number of input lines, it can return some illegal line count like −1 if too much input is presented. The output routine only has to print the lines in the order in which they appear in the array of pointers.

```
#define NULL    0
#define LINES   100  /* max lines to be sorted */

main()    /* sort input lines */
{
    char *lineptr[LINES]; /* pointers to text lines */
    int  nlines;         /* number of input lines read */

    if ((nlines = readlines(lineptr, LINES)) >= 0) {
        sort(lineptr, nlines);
        writelines(lineptr, nlines);
    }
    else
        printf("input too big to sort\n");
}
```

```
#define MAXLEN   1000

readlines(lineptr, maxlines)   /* read input lines */
char *lineptr[];               /* for sorting */
int maxlines;
{
     int  len, nlines;
     char *p, *alloc(), line[MAXLEN];

     nlines = 0;
     while ((len = getline(line, MAXLEN)) > 0)
          if (nlines >= maxlines)
               return(-1);
          else if ((p = alloc(len)) == NULL)
               return(-1);
          else {
               line[len-1] = '\0'; /* zap newline */
               strcpy(p, line);
               lineptr[nlines++] = p;
          }
     return(nlines);
}
```

The newline at the end of each line is deleted so it will not affect the order in which the lines are sorted.

```
writelines(lineptr, nlines)    /* write output lines */
char *lineptr[];
int nlines;
{
     int i;

     for (i = 0; i < nlines; i++)
          printf("%s\n", lineptr[i]);
}
```

The main new thing is the declaration for `lineptr`:

```
char *lineptr[LINES];
```

says that `lineptr` is an array of `LINES` elements, each element of which is a pointer to a `char`. That is, `lineptr[i]` is a character pointer, and `*lineptr[i]` accesses a character.

Since `lineptr` is itself an array which is passed to `writelines`, it can be treated as a pointer in exactly the same manner as our earlier examples, and the function can be written instead as

```
writelines(lineptr, nlines)    /* write output lines */
char *lineptr[];
int nlines;
{
      while (--nlines >= 0)
            printf("%s\n", *lineptr++);
}
```

*lineptr points initially to the first line; each increment advances it to the next line while nlines is counted down.

With input and output under control, we can proceed to sorting. The Shell sort from Chapter 3 needs minor changes: the declarations have to be modified, and the comparison operation must be moved into a separate function. The basic algorithm remains the same, which gives us some confidence that it will still work.

```
sort(v, n)     /* sort strings v[0] ... v[n-1] */
char *v[];            /* into increasing order */
int n;
{
      int gap, i, j;
      char *temp;

      for (gap = n/2; gap > 0; gap /= 2)
            for (i = gap; i < n; i++)
                  for (j = i-gap; j >= 0; j -= gap) {
                        if (strcmp(v[j], v[j+gap]) <= 0)
                              break;
                        temp = v[j];
                        v[j] = v[j+gap];
                        v[j+gap] = temp;
                  }
}
```

Since any individual element of v (alias lineptr) is a character pointer, temp also should be, so one can be copied to the other.

We wrote the program about as straightforwardly as possible, so as to get it working quickly. It might be faster, for instance, to copy the incoming lines directly into an array maintained by readlines, rather than copying them into line and then to a hidden place maintained by alloc. But it's wiser to make the first draft something easy to understand, and worry about "efficiency" later. The way to make this program significantly faster is probably not by avoiding an unnecessary copy of the input lines. Replacing the Shell sort by something better, like Quicksort, is more likely to make a difference.

In Chapter 1 we pointed out that because while and for loops test the termination condition *before* executing the loop body even once, they help to ensure that programs will work at their boundaries, in particular with no input. It is illuminating to walk through the functions of the sorting program, checking what happens if there is no input text at all.

Exercise 5-5. Rewrite `readlines` to create lines in an array supplied by `main`, rather than calling `alloc` to maintain storage. How much faster is the program? □

5.9   Initialization of Pointer Arrays

Consider the problem of writing a function `month_name(n)`, which returns a pointer to a character string containing the name of the n-th month. This is an ideal application for an internal `static` array. `month_name` contains a private array of character strings, and returns a pointer to the proper one when called. The topic of this section is how that array of names is initialized.

The syntax is quite similar to previous initializations:

```
char *month_name(n) /* return name of n-th month */
int n;
{
        static char *name[] ={
                "illegal month",
                "January",
                "February",
                "March",
                "April",
                "May",
                "June",
                "July",
                "August",
                "September",
                "October",
                "November",
                "December"
        };

        return((n < 1 || n > 12) ? name[0] : name[n]);
}
```

The declaration of `name`, which is an array of character pointers, is the same as `lineptr` in the sorting example. The initializer is simply a list of character strings; each is assigned to the corresponding position in the array. More precisely, the characters of the i-th string are placed somewhere else, and a pointer to them is stored in `name[i]`. Since the size of the array `name` is not specified, the compiler itself counts the initializers and fills in the correct number.

5.10   Pointers vs. Multi-dimensional Arrays

Newcomers to C are sometimes confused about the difference between a two-dimensional array and an array of pointers, such as `name` in the example above. Given the declarations

```
int a[10][10];
int *b[10];
```

the usage of `a` and `b` may be similar, in that `a[5][5]` and `b[5][5]` are both legal references to a single `int`. But `a` is a true array: all 100 storage cells have been allocated, and the conventional rectangular subscript calculation is done to find any given element. For `b`, however, the declaration only allocates 10 pointers; each must be set to point to an array of integers. Assuming that each does point to a ten-element array, then there will be 100 storage cells set aside, plus the ten cells for the pointers. Thus the array of pointers uses slightly more space, and may require an explicit initialization step. But it has two advantages: accessing an element is done by indirection through a pointer rather than by a multiplication and an addition, and the rows of the array may be of different lengths. That is, each element of `b` need not point to a ten-element vector; some may point to two elements, some to twenty, and some to none at all.

Although we have phrased this discussion in terms of integers, by far the most frequent use of arrays of pointers is like that shown in `month_name`: to store character strings of diverse lengths.

Exercise 5-6. Rewrite the routines `day_of_year` and `month_day` with pointers instead of indexing. □

5.11   Command-line Arguments

In environments that support C, there is a way to pass command-line arguments or parameters to a program when it begins executing. When `main` is called to begin execution, it is called with two arguments. The first (conventionally called `argc`) is the number of command-line arguments the program was invoked with; the second (`argv`) is a pointer to an array of character strings that contain the arguments, one per string. Manipulating these character strings is a common use of multiple levels of pointers.

The simplest illustration of the necessary declarations and use is the program `echo`, which simply echoes its command-line arguments on a single line, separated by blanks. That is, if the command

```
echo hello, world
```

is given, the output is

```
hello, world
```

By convention, `argv[0]` is the name by which the program was invoked, so `argc` is at least 1. In the example above, `argc` is 3, and `argv[0]`, `argv[1]` and `argv[2]` are "echo", "hello,", and "world" respectively. The first real argument is `argv[1]` and the last is `argv[argc-1]`. If `argc` is 1, there are no command-line arguments after the program name. This is shown in `echo`:

```
main(argc, argv)     /* echo arguments; 1st version */
int argc;
char *argv[];
{
        int i;

        for (i = 1; i < argc; i++)
                printf("%s%c", argv[i], (i<argc-1) ? ' ' : '\n');
}
```

Since `argv` is a pointer to an array of pointers, there are several ways to write this program that involve manipulating the pointer rather than indexing an array. Let us show two variations.

```
main(argc, argv)     /* echo arguments; 2nd version */
int argc;
char *argv[];
{
        while (--argc > 0)
                printf("%s%c", *++argv, (argc > 1) ? ' ' : '\n');
}
```

Since `argv` is a pointer to the beginning of the array of argument strings, incrementing it by 1 (`++argv`) makes it point at the original `argv[1]` instead of `argv[0]`. Each successive increment moves it along to the next argument; `*argv` is then the pointer to that argument. At the same time, `argc` is decremented; when it becomes zero, there are no arguments left to print.

Alternatively,

```
main(argc, argv)     /* echo arguments; 3rd version */
int argc;
char *argv[];
{
        while (--argc > 0)
                printf((argc > 1) ? "%s " : "%s\n", *++argv);
}
```

This version shows that the format argument of `printf` can be an expression just like any of the others. This usage is not very frequent, but worth remembering.

As a second example, let us make some enhancements to the pattern-finding program from Chapter 4. If you recall, we wired the search pattern deep into the program, an obviously unsatisfactory arrangement. Following the lead of the UNIX utility *grep*, let us change the program so the pattern to be matched is specified by the first argument on the command line.

```
#define   MAXLINE   1000

main(argc, argv)   /* find pattern from first argument */
int argc;
char *argv[];
{
      char line[MAXLINE];

      if (argc != 2)
            printf("Usage: find pattern\n");
      else
            while (getline(line, MAXLINE) > 0)
                  if (index(line, argv[1]) >= 0)
                        printf("%s", line);
}
```

The basic model can now be elaborated to illustrate further pointer constructions. Suppose we want to allow two optional arguments. One says "print all lines *except* those that match the pattern;" the second says "precede each printed line with its line number."

A common convention for C programs is that an argument beginning with a minus sign introduces an optional flag or parameter. If we choose −x (for "except") to signal the inversion, and −n ("number") to request line numbering, then the command

```
find   −x   −n   the
```

with the input

```
now is the time
for all good men
to come to the aid
of their party.
```

should produce the output

```
2: for all good men
```

Optional arguments should be permitted in any order, and the rest of the program should be insensitive to the number of arguments which were actually present. In particular, the call to index should not refer to argv[2] when there was a single flag argument and to argv[1] when there wasn't. Furthermore, it is convenient for users if option arguments can be concatenated, as in

        find -nx the

Here is the program.

```
        #define    MAXLINE    1000

    main(argc, argv)   /* find pattern from first argument */
    int argc;
    char *argv[];
    {
        char line[MAXLINE], *s;
        long lineno = 0;
        int  except = 0, number = 0;

        while (--argc > 0 && (*++argv)[0] == '-')
            for (s = argv[0]+1; *s != '\0'; s++)
                switch (*s) {
                case 'x':
                    except = 1;
                    break;
                case 'n':
                    number = 1;
                    break;
                default:
                    printf("find: illegal option %c\n", *s);
                    argc = 0;
                    break;
                }
        if (argc != 1)
            printf("Usage: find -x -n pattern\n");
        else
            while (getline(line, MAXLINE) > 0) {
                lineno++;
                if ((index(line, *argv) >= 0) != except) {
                    if (number)
                        printf("%ld: ", lineno);
                    printf("%s", line);
                }
            }
    }
```

argv is incremented before each optional argument, and argc decremented. If there are no errors, at the end of the loop argc should be 1 and *argv should point at the pattern. Notice that *++argv is a pointer to an argument string; (*++argv)[0] is its first character. The parentheses are necessary, for without them the expression would be *++(argv[0]), which is quite different (and wrong). An alternate valid form would be

`**++argv`.

Exercise 5-7. Write the program `add` which evaluates a reverse Polish expression from the command line. For example,

```
add   2   3   4   +   *
```

evaluates $2 \times (3+4)$. □

Exercise 5-8. Modify the programs `entab` and `detab` (written as exercises in Chapter 1) to accept a list of tab stops as arguments. Use the normal tab settings if there are no arguments. □

Exercise 5-9. Extend `entab` and `detab` to accept the shorthand

```
entab  m +n
```

to mean tabs stops every *n* columns, starting at column *m*. Choose convenient (for the user) default behavior. □

Exercise 5-10. Write the program `tail`, which prints the last *n* lines of its input. By default, *n* is 10, let us say, but it can be changed by an optional argument, so that

```
tail −n
```

prints the last *n* lines. The program should behave rationally no matter how unreasonable the input or the value of *n*. Write the program so it makes the best use of available storage: lines should be stored as in `sort`, not in a two-dimensional array of fixed size. □

5.12   Pointers to Functions

In C, a function itself is not a variable, but it is possible to define a *pointer to a function*, which can be manipulated, passed to functions, placed in arrays, and so on. We will illustrate this by modifying the sorting procedure written earlier in this chapter so that if the optional argument −n is given, it will sort the input lines numerically instead of lexicographically.

A sort often consists of three parts — a *comparison* which determines the ordering of any pair of objects, an *exchange* which reverses their order, and a *sorting algorithm* which makes comparisons and exchanges until the objects are in order. The sorting algorithm is independent of the comparison and exchange operations, so by passing different comparison and exchange functions to it, we can arrange to sort by different criteria. This is the approach taken in our new sort.

The lexicographic comparison of two lines is done by `strcmp` and swapping by `swap` as before; we will also need a routine `numcmp` which compares two lines on the basis of numeric value and returns the same kind of condition indication as `strcmp` does. These three functions are declared in

main and pointers to them are passed to sort. sort in turn calls the
functions via the pointers. We have skimped on error processing for arguments, so as to concentrate on the main issues.

```
#define LINES 100   /* max number of lines to be sorted */

main(argc, argv)      /* sort input lines */
int argc;
char *argv[];
{
        char *lineptr[LINES];   /* pointers to text lines */
        int  nlines;          /* number of input lines read */
        int  strcmp(), numcmp(); /* comparison functions */
        int  swap();   /* exchange function */
        int  numeric = 0;   /* 1 if numeric sort */

        if (argc>1 && argv[1][0] == '-' && argv[1][1] == 'n')
             numeric = 1;
        if ((nlines = readlines(lineptr, LINES)) >= 0) {
             if (numeric)
                   sort(lineptr, nlines, numcmp, swap);
             else
                   sort(lineptr, nlines, strcmp, swap);
             writelines(lineptr, nlines);
        } else
             printf("input too big to sort\n");
}
```

strcmp, numcmp and swap are addresses of functions; since they are
known to be functions, the & operator is not necessary, in the same way that
it is not needed before an array name. The compiler arranges for the
address of the function to be passed.
    The second step is to modify sort:

```
sort(v, n, comp, exch)    /* sort strings v[0]...v[n-1] */
char *v[];                /* into increasing order */
int n;
int (*comp)(), (*exch)();
{
    int gap, i, j;

    for (gap = n/2; gap > 0; gap /= 2)
        for (i = gap; i < n; i++)
            for (j = i-gap; j >= 0; j -= gap) {
                if ((*comp)(v[j], v[j+gap]) <= 0)
                    break;
                (*exch)(&v[j], &v[j+gap]);
            }
}
```

The declarations should be studied with some care.

```
int (*comp)()
```

says that comp is a pointer to a function that returns an int. The first set of parentheses are necessary; without them,

```
int *comp()
```

would say that comp is a function returning a pointer to an int, which is quite a different thing.

The use of comp in the line

```
if ((*comp)(v[j], v[j+gap]) <= 0)
```

is consistent with the declaration: comp is a pointer to a function, *comp is the function, and

```
(*comp)(v[j], v[j+gap])
```

is the call to it. The parentheses are needed so the components are correctly associated.

We have already shown strcmp, which compares two strings. Here is numcmp, which compares two strings on a leading numeric value:

```
numcmp(s1, s2) /* compare s1 and s2 numerically */
char *s1, *s2;
{
    double atof(), v1, v2;

    v1 = atof(s1);
    v2 = atof(s2);
    if (v1 < v2)
        return(-1);
    else if (v1 > v2)
        return(1);
    else
        return(0);
}
```

The final step is to add the function `swap` which exchanges two pointers. This is adapted directly from what we presented early in the chapter.

```
swap(px, py)    /* interchange *px and *py */
char *px[], *py[];
{
    char *temp;

    temp = *px;
    *px = *py;
    *py = temp;
}
```

There are a variety of other options that can be added to the sorting program; some make challenging exercises.

Exercise 5-11. Modify `sort` to handle a −r flag, which indicates sorting in reverse (decreasing) order. Of course −r must work with −n. □

Exercise 5-12. Add the option −f to fold upper and lower case together, so that case distinctions are not made during sorting: upper and lower case data are sorted together, so that a and A appear adjacent, not separated by an entire case of the alphabet. □

Exercise 5-13. Add the −d ("dictionary order") option, which makes comparisons only on letters, numbers and blanks. Make sure it works in conjunction with −f. □

Exercise 5-14. Add a field-handling capability, so sorting may be done on fields within lines, each field according to an independent set of options. (The index for this book was sorted with −df for the index category and −n for the page numbers.) □

CHAPTER 6: **STRUCTURES**

A *structure* is a collection of one or more variables, possibly of different types, grouped together under a single name for convenient handling. (Structures are called "records" in some languages, most notably Pascal.)

The traditional example of a structure is the payroll record: an "employee" is described by a set of attributes such as name, address, social security number, salary, etc. Some of these in turn could be structures: a name has several components, as does an address and even a salary.

Structures help to organize complicated data, particularly in large programs, because in many situations they permit a group of related variables to be treated as a unit instead of as separate entities. In this chapter we will try to illustrate how structures are used. The programs we will use are bigger than many of the others in the book, but still of modest size.

6.1 Basics

Let us revisit the date conversion routines of Chapter 5. A date consists of several parts, such as the day, month, and year, and perhaps the day of the year and the month name. These five variables can all be placed into a single structure like this:

```
struct date {
    int  day;
    int  month;
    int  year;
    int  yearday;
    char mon_name[4];
};
```

The keyword struct introduces a structure declaration, which is a list of declarations enclosed in braces. An optional name called a *structure tag* may follow the word struct (as with date here). The tag names this kind of structure, and can be used subsequently as a shorthand for the detailed declaration.

119

The elements or variables mentioned in a structure are called *members*. A structure member or tag and an ordinary (i.e., non-member) variable can have the same name without conflict, since they can always be distinguished by context. Of course as a matter of style one would normally use the same names only for closely related objects.

The right brace that terminates the list of members may be followed by a list of variables, just as for any basic type. That is,

```
struct { ... } x, y, z;
```

is syntactically analogous to

```
int x, y, z;
```

in the sense that each statement declares x, y and z to be variables of the named type and causes space to be allocated for them.

A structure declaration that is not followed by a list of variables allocates no storage; it merely describes a *template* or the shape of a structure. If the declaration is tagged, however, the tag can be used later in definitions of actual instances of the structure. For example, given the declaration of date above,

```
struct date d;
```

defines a variable d which is a structure of type date. An external or static structure can be initialized by following its definition with a list of initializers for the components:

```
struct date d ={ 4, 7, 1776, 186, "Jul" };
```

A member of a particular structure is referred to in an expression by a construction of the form

structure-name . member

The structure member operator "." connects the structure name and the member name. To set leap from the date in structure d, for example,

```
leap = d.year % 4 == 0 && d.year % 100 != 0
            || d.year % 400 == 0;
```

or to check the month name,

```
if (strcmp(d.mon_name, "Aug") == 0) ...
```

or to convert the first character of the month name to lower case,

```
d.mon_name[0] = lower(d.mon_name[0]);
```

Structures can be nested; a payroll record might actually look like

```
        struct person {
              char name[NAMESIZE];
              char address[ADRSIZE];
              long zipcode;
              long ss_number;
              double salary;
              struct date birthdate;
              struct date hiredate;
        };
```

The `person` structure contains two dates. If we declare `emp` as

```
        struct person emp;
```

then

```
        emp.birthdate.month
```

refers to the month of birth. The structure member operator `.` associates left to right.

6.2   Structures and Functions

There are a number of restrictions on C structures. The essential rules are that the only operations that you can perform on a structure are take its address with `&`, and access one of its members. This implies that structures may not be assigned to or copied as a unit, and that they can not be passed to or returned from functions. (These restrictions will be removed in forthcoming versions.) Pointers to structures do not suffer these limitations, however, so structures and functions do work together comfortably. Finally, automatic structures, like automatic arrays, cannot be initialized; only external or static structures can.

Let us investigate some of these points by rewriting the date conversion functions of the last chapter to use structures. Since the rules prohibit passing a structure to a function directly, we must either pass the components separately, or pass a pointer to the whole thing. The first alternative uses `day_of_year` as we wrote it in Chapter 5:

```
        d.yearday = day_of_year(d.year, d.month, d.day);
```

The other way is to pass a pointer. If we have declared `hiredate` as

```
        struct date hiredate;
```

and re-written `day_of_year`, we can then say

```
        hiredate.yearday = day_of_year(&hiredate);
```

to pass a pointer to `hiredate` to `day_of_year`. The function has to be modified because its argument is now a pointer rather than a list of variables.

```
day_of_year(pd)    /* set day of year from month, day */
struct date *pd;
{
      int i, day, leap;

      day = pd->day;
      leap = pd->year % 4 == 0 && pd->year % 100 != 0
                || pd->year % 400 == 0;
      for (i = 1; i < pd->month; i++)
            day += day_tab[leap][i];
      return(day);
}
```

The declaration

```
struct date *pd;
```

says that `pd` is a pointer to a structure of type `date`. The notation exemplified by

```
pd->year
```

is new. If `p` is a pointer to a structure, then

```
p->member-of-structure
```

refers to the particular member. (The operator `->` is a minus sign followed by `>`.)

Since `pd` points to the structure, the `year` member could also be referred to as

```
(*pd).year
```

but pointers to structures are so frequently used that the `->` notation is provided as a convenient shorthand. The parentheses are necessary in `(*pd).year` because the precedence of the structure member operator `.` is higher than `*`. Both `->` and `.` associate from left to right, so

```
p->q->memb
emp.birthdate.month
```

are

```
(p->q)->memb
(emp.birthdate).month
```

For completeness here is the other function, `month_day`, rewritten to use the structure.

```
month_day(pd)   /* set month and day from day of year */
struct date *pd;
{
      int i, leap;

      leap = pd->year % 4 == 0 && pd->year % 100 != 0
                  || pd->year % 400 == 0;
      pd->day = pd->yearday;
      for (i = 1; pd->day > day_tab[leap][i]; i++)
            pd->day -= day_tab[leap][i];
      pd->month = i;
}
```

The structure operators -> and ., together with () for argument lists and [] for subscripts, are at the top of the precedence hierarchy and thus bind very tightly. For example, given the declaration

```
struct {
      int  x;
      int  *y;
} *p;
```

then

```
++p->x
```

increments x, not p, because the implied parenthesization is ++(p->x). Parentheses can be used to alter the binding: (++p)->x increments p before accessing x, and (p++)->x increments p afterward. (This last set of parentheses is unnecessary. Why?)

In the same way, *p->y fetches whatever y points to; *p->y++ increments y after accessing whatever it points to (just like *s++); (*p->y)++ increments whatever y points to; and *p++->y increments p after accessing whatever y points to.

6.3 Arrays of Structures

Structures are especially suitable for managing arrays of related variables. For instance, consider a program to count the occurrences of each C keyword. We need an array of character strings to hold the names, and an array of integers for the counts. One possibility is to use two parallel arrays keyword and keycount, as in

```
char *keyword[NKEYS];
int  keycount[NKEYS];
```

But the very fact that the arrays are parallel indicates that a different organization is possible. Each keyword entry is really a pair:

```
    char *keyword;
    int  keycount;
```

and there is an array of pairs. The structure declaration

```
struct key {
    char *keyword;
    int  keycount;
} keytab[NKEYS];
```

defines an array `keytab` of structures of this type, and allocates storage to them. Each element of the array is a structure. This could also be written

```
struct key {
    char *keyword;
    int  keycount;
};
```

```
struct key keytab[NKEYS];
```

Since the structure `keytab` actually contains a constant set of names, it is easiest to initialize it once and for all when it is defined. The structure initialization is quite analogous to earlier ones — the definition is followed by a list of initializers enclosed in braces:

```
struct key {
    char *keyword;
    int  keycount;
} keytab[] ={
    "break", 0,
    "case", 0,
    "char", 0,
    "continue", 0,
    "default", 0,
    /* ... */
    "unsigned", 0,
    "while", 0
};
```

The initializers are listed in pairs corresponding to the structure members. It would be more precise to enclose initializers for each "row" or structure in braces, as in

```
{ "break", 0 },
{ "case", 0 },
...
```

but the inner braces are not necessary when the initializers are simple variables or character strings, and when all are present. As usual, the compiler will compute the number of entries in the array `keytab` if initializers are present and the `[]` is left empty.

The keyword-counting program begins with the definition of `keytab`. The main routine reads the input by repeatedly calling a function `getword` that fetches the input one word at a time. Each word is looked up in `keytab` with a version of the binary search function that we wrote in Chapter 3. (Of course the list of keywords has to be given in increasing order for this to work.)

```
#define   MAXWORD   20

main()    /* count C keywords */
{
    int   n, t;
    char word[MAXWORD];

    while ((t = getword(word, MAXWORD)) != EOF)
        if (t == LETTER)
            if ((n = binary(word, keytab, NKEYS)) >= 0)
                keytab[n].keycount++;
    for (n = 0; n < NKEYS; n++)
        if (keytab[n].keycount > 0)
            printf("%4d %s\n",
                keytab[n].keycount, keytab[n].keyword);
}

binary(word, tab, n)   /* find word in tab[0]...tab[n-1] */
char *word;
struct key tab[];
int n;
{
    int low, high, mid, cond;

    low = 0;
    high = n - 1;
    while (low <= high) {
        mid = (low+high) / 2;
        if ((cond = strcmp(word, tab[mid].keyword)) < 0)
            high = mid - 1;
        else if (cond > 0)
            low = mid + 1;
        else
            return(mid);
    }
    return(-1);
}
```

We will show the function `getword` in a moment; for now it suffices to say that it returns LETTER each time it finds a word, and copies the word into its first argument.

The quantity **NKEYS** is the number of keywords in **keytab**. Although we could count this by hand, it's a lot easier and safer to do it by machine, especially if the list is subject to change. One possibility would be to terminate the list of initializers with a null pointer, then loop along **keytab** until the end is found.

But this is more than is needed, since the size of the array is completely determined at compile time. The number of entries is just

   size of **keytab** / *size of* **struct key**

C provides a compile-time unary operator called **sizeof** which can be used to compute the size of any object. The expression

   sizeof (*object*)

yields an integer equal to the size of the specified object. (The size is given in unspecified units called "bytes," which are the same size as a **char**.) The object can be an actual variable or array or structure, or the name of a basic type like **int** or **double**, or the name of a derived type like a structure. In our case, the number of keywords is the array size divided by the size of one array element. This computation is used in a **#define** statement to set the value of **NKEYS**:

```
#define  NKEYS  (sizeof(keytab) / sizeof(struct key))
```

Now for the function **getword**. We have actually written a more general **getword** than is necessary for this program, but it is not really much more complicated. **getword** returns the next "word" from the input, where a word is either a string of letters and digits beginning with a letter, or a single character. The type of the object is returned as a function value; it is **LETTER** if the token is a word, **EOF** for end of file, or the character itself if it is non-alphabetic.

```
    getword(w, lim)       /* get next word from input */
    char *w;
    int lim;
    {
        int c, t;

        if (type(c = *w++ = getch()) != LETTER) {
            *w = '\0';
            return(c);
        }
        while (--lim > 0) {
            t = type(c = *w++ = getch());
            if (t != LETTER && t != DIGIT) {
                ungetch(c);
                break;
            }
        }
        *(w-1) = '\0';
        return(LETTER);
    }
```

getword uses the routines getch and ungetch which we wrote in
Chapter 4: when the collection of an alphabetic token stops, getword has
gone one character too far. The call to ungetch pushes that character back
on the input for the next call.

getword calls type to determine the type of each individual character
of input. Here is a version *for the ASCII alphabet only.*

```
    type(c)     /* return type of ASCII character */
    int c;
    {
        if (c >= 'a' && c <= 'z' || c >= 'A' && c <= 'Z')
            return(LETTER);
        else if (c >= '0' && c <= '9')
            return(DIGIT);
        else
            return(c);
    }
```

The symbolic constants LETTER and DIGIT can have any values that do
not conflict with non-alphanumeric characters and EOF; the obvious choices
are

```
    #define    LETTER    'a'
    #define    DIGIT     '0'
```

getword can be faster if calls to the function type are replaced by
references to an appropriate array type[]. The standard C library provides
macros called isalpha and isdigit which operate in this manner.

Exercise 6-1. Make this modification to `getword` and measure the change in speed of the program. □

Exercise 6-2. Write a version of `type` which is independent of character set. □

Exercise 6-3. Write a version of the keyword-counting program which does not count occurrences contained within quoted strings. □

6.4   Pointers to Structures

To illustrate some of the considerations involved with pointers and arrays of structures, let us write the keyword-counting program again, this time using pointers instead of array indices.

The external declaration of `keytab` need not change, but `main` and `binary` do need modification.

```
main()     /* count C keywords; pointer version */
{
    int  t;
    char word[MAXWORD];
    struct key *binary(), *p;

    while ((t = getword(word, MAXWORD)) != EOF)
        if (t == LETTER)
            if ((p=binary(word, keytab, NKEYS)) != NULL)
                p->keycount++;
    for (p = keytab; p < keytab + NKEYS; p++)
        if (p->keycount > 0)
            printf("%4d %s\n", p->keycount, p->keyword);
}
```

```
struct key *binary(word, tab, n) /* find word */
char *word;                /* in tab[0]...tab[n-1] */
struct key tab[];
int n;
{
    int  cond;
    struct key *low = &tab[0];
    struct key *high = &tab[n-1];
    struct key *mid;

    while (low <= high) {
        mid = low + (high-low) / 2;
        if ((cond = strcmp(word, mid->keyword)) < 0)
            high = mid - 1;
        else if (cond > 0)
            low = mid + 1;
        else
            return(mid);
    }
    return(NULL);
}
```

There are several things worthy of note here. First, the declaration of binary must indicate that it returns a pointer to the structure type key, instead of an integer; this is declared both in main and in binary. If binary finds the word, it returns a pointer to it; if it fails, it returns NULL.

Second, all the accessing of elements of keytab is done by pointers. This causes one significant change in binary: the computation of the middle element can no longer be simply

```
mid = (low+high) / 2
```

because the *addition* of two pointers will not produce any kind of a useful answer (even when divided by 2), and in fact is illegal. This must be changed to

```
mid = low + (high-low) / 2
```

which sets mid to point to the element halfway between low and high.

You should also study the initializers for low and high. It is possible to initialize a pointer to the address of a previously defined object; that is precisely what we have done here.

In main we wrote

```
for (p = keytab; p < keytab + NKEYS; p++)
```

If p is a pointer to a structure, any arithmetic on p takes into account the actual size of the structure, so p++ increments p by the correct amount to get the next element of the array of structures. But don't assume that the size of a structure is the sum of the sizes of its members — because of alignment requirements for different objects, there may be "holes" in a structure.

Finally, an aside on program format. When a function returns a complicated type, as in

```
struct key *binary(word, tab, n)
```

the function name can be hard to see, and to find with a text editor. Accordingly an alternate style is sometimes used:

```
struct key *
binary(word, tab, n)
```

This is mostly a matter of personal taste; pick the form you like and hold to it.

6.5 Self-referential Structures

Suppose we want to handle the more general problem of counting the occurrences of *all* the words in some input. Since the list of words isn't known in advance, we can't conveniently sort it and use a binary search. Yet we can't do a linear search for each word as it arrives, to see if it's already been seen; the program would take forever. (More precisely, its expected running time would grow quadratically with the number of input words.) How can we organize the data to cope efficiently with a list of arbitrary words?

One solution is to keep the set of words seen so far sorted at all times, by placing each word into its proper position in the order as it arrives. This shouldn't be done by shifting words in a linear array, though — that also takes too long. Instead we will use a data structure called a *binary tree*.

The tree contains one "node" per distinct word; each node contains

> *a pointer to the text of the word*
> *a count of the number of occurrences*
> *a pointer to the left child node*
> *a pointer to the right child node*

No node may have more than two children; it might have only zero or one.

The nodes are maintained so that at any node the left subtree contains only words which are less than the word at the node, and the right subtree contains only words that are greater. To find out whether a new word is already in the tree, one starts at the root and compares the new word to the word stored at that node. If they match, the question is answered affirmatively. If the new word is less than the tree word, the search continues at the left child; otherwise the right child is investigated. If there is no child in the required direction, the new word is not in the tree, and in fact the proper place for it to be is the missing child. This search process is inherently recursive, since the search from any node uses a search from one of its children. Accordingly recursive routines for insertion and printing will be most natural.

Going back to the description of a node, it is clearly a structure with four components:

```
struct tnode {        /* the basic node */
     char *word;       /* points to the text */
     int  count;       /* number of occurrences */
     struct tnode *left;      /* left child */
     struct tnode *right;      /* right child */
};
```

This "recursive" declaration of a node might look chancy, but it's actually quite correct. It is illegal for a structure to contain an instance of itself, but

```
struct tnode *left;
```

declares `left` to be a *pointer* to a node, not a node itself.

The code for the whole program is surprisingly small, given a handful of supporting routines that we have already written. These are `getword`, to fetch each input word, and `alloc`, to provide space for squirreling the words away.

The main routine simply reads words with `getword` and installs them in the tree with `tree`.

```
#define   MAXWORD   20

main()    /* word frequency count */
{
     struct tnode *root, *tree();
     char word[MAXWORD];
     int  t;

     root = NULL;
     while ((t = getword(word, MAXWORD)) != EOF)
          if (t == LETTER)
               root = tree(root, word);
     treeprint(root);
}
```

`tree` itself is straightforward. A word is presented by `main` to the top level (the root) of the tree. At each stage, that word is compared to the word already stored at the node, and is percolated down to either the left or right subtree by a recursive call to `tree`. Eventually the word either matches something already in the tree (in which case the count is incremented), or a null pointer is encountered, indicating that a node must be created and added to the tree. If a new node is created, `tree` returns a pointer to it, which is installed in the parent node.

```
struct tnode *tree(p, w) /* install w at or below p */
struct tnode *p;
char *w;
{
    struct tnode *talloc();
    char *strsave();
    int  cond;

    if (p == NULL) {    /* a new word has arrived */
        p = talloc();   /* make a new node */
        p->word = strsave(w);
        p->count = 1;
        p->left = p->right = NULL;
    } else if ((cond = strcmp(w, p->word)) == 0)
        p->count++;     /* repeated word */
    else if (cond < 0)  /* lower goes into left subtree */
        p->left = tree(p->left, w);
    else                /* greater into right subtree */
        p->right = tree(p->right, w);
    return(p);
}
```

Storage for the new node is fetched by a routine `talloc`, which is an adaptation of the `alloc` we wrote earlier. It returns a pointer to a free space suitable for holding a tree node. (We will discuss this more in a moment.) The new word is copied to a hidden place by `strsave`, the count is initialized, and the two children are made null. This part of the code is executed only at the edge of the tree, when a new node is being added. We have (unwisely for a production program) omitted error checking on the values returned by `strsave` and `talloc`.

`treeprint` prints the tree in left subtree order; at each node, it prints the left subtree (all the words less than this word), then the word itself, then the right subtree (all the words greater). If you feel shaky about recursion, draw yourself a tree and print it with `treeprint`; it's one of the cleanest recursive routines you can find.

```
        treeprint(p)    /* print tree p recursively */
        struct tnode *p;
        {
            if (p != NULL) {
                treeprint(p->left);
                printf("%4d %s\n", p->count, p->word);
                treeprint(p->right);
            }
        }
```

A practical note: if the tree becomes "unbalanced" because the words don't arrive in random order, the running time of the program can grow too fast. As a worst case, if the words are already in order, this program does an expensive simulation of linear search. There are generalizations of the binary tree, notably 2-3 trees and AVL trees, which do not suffer from this worst-case behavior, but we will not describe them here.

Before we leave this example, it is also worth a brief digression on a problem related to storage allocators. Clearly it's desirable that there be only one storage allocator in a program, even though it allocates different kinds of objects. But if one allocator is to process requests for, say, pointers to char's and pointers to struct tnode's, two questions arise. First, how does it meet the requirement of most real machines that objects of certain types must satisfy alignment restrictions (for example, integers often must be located on even addresses)? Second, what declarations can cope with the fact that alloc necessarily returns different kinds of pointers?

Alignment requirements can generally be satisfied easily, at the cost of some wasted space, merely by ensuring that the allocator always returns a pointer that meets *all* alignment restrictions. For example, on the PDP-11 it is sufficient that alloc always return an even pointer, since any type of object may be stored at an even address. The only cost is a wasted character on odd-length requests. Similar actions are taken on other machines. Thus the implementation of alloc may not be portable, but the usage is. The alloc of Chapter 5 does not guarantee any particular alignment; in Chapter 8 we will show how to do the job right.

The question of the type declaration for alloc is a vexing one for any language that takes its type-checking seriously. In C, the best procedure is to declare that alloc returns a pointer to char, then explicitly coerce the pointer into the desired type with a cast. That is, if p is declared as

```
        char *p;
```

then

```
        (struct tnode *) p
```

converts it into a tnode pointer in an expression. Thus talloc is written as

```
struct tnode *talloc()
{
      char *alloc();

      return((struct tnode *) alloc(sizeof(struct tnode)));
}
```

This is more than is needed for current compilers, but represents the safest course for the future.

Exercise 6-4. Write a program which reads a C program and prints in alphabetical order each group of variable names which are identical in the first 7 characters, but different somewhere thereafter. (Make sure that 7 is a parameter). □

Exercise 6-5. Write a basic cross-referencer: a program which prints a list of all words in a document, and, for each word, a list of the line numbers on which it occurs. □

Exercise 6-6. Write a program which prints the distinct words in its input sorted into decreasing order of frequency of occurrence. Precede each word by its count. □

6.6   Table Lookup

In this section we will write the innards of a table-lookup package as an illustration of more aspects of structures. This code is typical of what might be found in the symbol table management routines of a macro processor or a compiler. For example, consider the C #define statement. When a line like

```
#define  YES  1
```

is encountered, the name YES and the replacement text 1 are stored in a table. Later, when the name YES appears in a statement like

```
inword = YES;
```

it must be replaced by 1.

There are two major routines that manipulate the names and replacement texts. install(s, t) records the name s and the replacement text t in a table; s and t are just character strings. lookup(s) searches for s in the table, and returns a pointer to the place where it was found, or NULL if it wasn't there.

The algorithm used is a hash search — the incoming name is converted into a small positive integer, which is then used to index into an array of pointers. An array element points to the beginning of a chain of blocks describing names that have that hash value. It is NULL if no names have hashed to that value.

A block in the chain is a structure containing pointers to the name, the replacement text, and the next block in the chain. A null next-pointer marks the end of the chain.

```
struct nlist { /* basic table entry */
     char *name;
     char *def;
     struct nlist *next; /* next entry in chain */
};
```

The pointer array is just

```
#define   HASHSIZE  100
static struct nlist *hashtab[HASHSIZE]; /* pointer table */
```

The hashing function, which is used by both lookup and install, simply adds up the character values in the string and forms the remainder modulo the array size. (This is not the best possible algorithm, but it has the merit of extreme simplicity.)

```
hash(s)    /* form hash value for string s */
char *s;
{
     int hashval;

     for (hashval = 0; *s != '\0'; )
          hashval += *s++;
     return(hashval % HASHSIZE);
}
```

The hashing process produces a starting index in the array hashtab; if the string is to be found anywhere, it will be in the chain of blocks beginning there. The search is performed by lookup. If lookup finds the entry already present, it returns a pointer to it; if not, it returns NULL.

```
struct nlist *lookup(s)   /* look for s in hashtab */
char *s;
{
     struct nlist *np;

     for (np = hashtab[hash(s)]; np != NULL; np = np->next)
          if (strcmp(s, np->name) == 0)
               return(np);      /* found it */
     return(NULL);   /* not found */
}
```

install uses lookup to determine whether the name being installed is already present; if so, the new definition must supersede the old one.

Otherwise, a completely new entry is created. `install` returns NULL if for any reason there is no room for a new entry.

```
struct nlist *install(name, def)    /* put (name, def) */
char *name, *def;                  /* in hashtab */
{
      struct nlist *np, *lookup();
      char *strsave(), *alloc();
      int  hashval;

      if ((np = lookup(name)) == NULL) { /* not found */
            np = (struct nlist *) alloc(sizeof(*np));
            if (np == NULL)
                  return(NULL);
            if ((np->name = strsave(name)) == NULL)
                  return(NULL);
            hashval = hash(np->name);
            np->next = hashtab[hashval];
            hashtab[hashval] = np;
      } else          /* already there */
            free(np->def); /* free previous definition */
      if ((np->def = strsave(def)) == NULL)
            return(NULL);
      return(np);
}
```

`strsave` merely copies the string given by its argument into a safe place, obtained by a call on `alloc`. We showed the code in Chapter 5. Since calls to `alloc` and `free` may occur in any order, and since alignment matters, the simple version of `alloc` in Chapter 5 is not adequate here; see Chapters 7 and 8.

Exercise 6-7. Write a routine which will remove a name and definition from the table maintained by `lookup` and `install`. □

Exercise 6-8. Implement a simple version of the `#define` processor suitable for use with C programs, based on the routines of this section. You may also find `getch` and `ungetch` helpful. □

6.7   Fields

When storage space is at a premium, it may be necessary to pack several objects into a single machine word; one especially common use is a set of single-bit flags in applications like compiler symbol tables. Externally-imposed data formats, such as interfaces to hardware devices, also often require the ability to get at pieces of a word.

Imagine a fragment of a compiler that manipulates a symbol table. Each identifier in a program has certain information associated with it, for example, whether or not it is a keyword, whether or not it is external and/or static, and so on. The most compact way to encode such information is a set of one-bit flags in a single `char` or `int`.

The usual way this is done is to define a set of "masks" corresponding to the relevant bit positions, as in

```
#define   KEYWORD    01
#define   EXTERNAL   02
#define   STATIC     04
```

(The numbers must be powers of two.) Then accessing the bits becomes a matter of "bit-fiddling" with the shifting, masking, and complementing operators which were described in Chapter 2.

Certain idioms appear frequently:

```
flags |= EXTERNAL | STATIC;
```

turns on the **EXTERNAL** and **STATIC** bits in `flags`, while

```
flags &= ~(EXTERNAL | STATIC);
```

turns them off, and

```
if ((flags & (EXTERNAL | STATIC)) == 0) ...
```

is true if both bits are off.

Although these idioms are readily mastered, as an alternative, C offers the capability of defining and accessing fields within a word directly rather than by bitwise logical operators. A *field* is a set of adjacent bits within a single `int`. The syntax of field definition and access is based on structures. For example, the symbol table `#define`'s above could be replaced by the definition of three fields:

```
struct {
    unsigned   is_keyword : 1;
    unsigned   is_extern : 1;
    unsigned   is_static : 1;
} flags;
```

This defines a variable called `flags` that contains three 1-bit fields. The number following the colon represents the field width in bits. The fields are declared `unsigned` to emphasize that they really are unsigned quantities.

Individual fields are referenced as `flags.is_keyword`, `flags.is_extern`, etc., just like other structure members. Fields behave like small, unsigned integers, and may participate in arithmetic expressions just like other integers. Thus the previous examples may be written more naturally as

```
        flags.is_extern = flags.is_static = 1;
```

to turn the bits on;

```
        flags.is_extern = flags.is_static = 0;
```

to turn them off; and

```
        if (flags.is_extern == 0 && flags.is_static == 0) ...
```

to test them.

A field may not overlap an `int` boundary; if the width would cause this to happen, the field is aligned at the next `int` boundary. Fields need not be named; unnamed fields (a colon and width only) are used for padding. The special width 0 may be used to force alignment at the next `int` boundary.

There are a number of caveats that apply to fields. Perhaps most significant, fields are assigned left to right on some machines and right to left on others, reflecting the nature of different hardware. This means that although fields are quite useful for maintaining internally-defined data structures, the question of which end comes first has to be carefully considered when picking apart externally-defined data.

Other restrictions to bear in mind: fields are unsigned; they may be stored only in `int`'s (or, equivalently, `unsigned`'s); they are not arrays; they do not have addresses, so the & operator cannot be applied to them.

6.8   Unions

A *union* is a variable which may hold (at different times) objects of different types and sizes, with the compiler keeping track of size and alignment requirements. Unions provide a way to manipulate different kinds of data in a single area of storage, without embedding any machine-dependent information in the program.

As an example, again from a compiler symbol table, suppose that constants may be `int`'s, `float`'s or character pointers. The value of a particular constant must be stored in a variable of the proper type, yet it is most convenient for table management if the value occupies the same amount of storage and is stored in the same place regardless of its type. This is the purpose of a union — to provide a single variable which can legitimately hold any one of several types. As with fields, the syntax is based on structures.

```
        union u_tag {
            int   ival;
            float fval;
            char *pval;
        } uval;
```

The variable `uval` will be large enough to hold the largest of the three types, regardless of the machine it is compiled on — the code is independent of hardware characteristics. Any one of these types may be assigned to `uval` and then used in expressions, so long as the usage is consistent: the type retrieved must be the type most recently stored. It is the responsibility of the programmer to keep track of what type is currently stored in a union; the results are machine dependent if something is stored as one type and extracted as another.

Syntactically, members of a union are accessed as

> *union-name . member*

or

> *union-pointer –> member*

just as for structures. If the variable `utype` is used to keep track of the current type stored in `uval`, then one might see code such as

```
if (utype == INT)
    printf("%d\n", uval.ival);
else if (utype == FLOAT)
    printf("%f\n", uval.fval);
else if (utype == STRING)
    printf("%s\n", uval.pval);
else
    printf("bad type %d in utype\n", utype);
```

Unions may occur within structures and arrays and vice versa. The notation for accessing a member of a union in a structure (or vice versa) is identical to that for nested structures. For example, in the structure array defined by

```
struct {
    char *name;
    int  flags;
    int  utype;
    union {
        int  ival;
        float fval;
        char *pval;
    } uval;
} symtab[NSYM];
```

the variable `ival` is referred to as

```
symtab[i].uval.ival
```

and the first character of the string `pval` by

```
*symtab[i].uval.pval
```

In effect, a union is a structure in which all members have offset zero, the structure is big enough to hold the "widest" member, and the alignment is appropriate for all of the types in the union. As with structures, the only operations currently permitted on unions are accessing a member and taking the address; unions may not be assigned to, passed to functions, or returned by functions. Pointers to unions can be used in a manner identical to pointers to structures.

The storage allocator in Chapter 8 shows how a union can be used to force a variable to be aligned on a particular kind of storage boundary.

6.9   Typedef

C provides a facility called `typedef` for creating new data type names. For example, the declaration

```
typedef int LENGTH;
```

makes the name `LENGTH` a synonym for `int`. The "type" `LENGTH` can be used in declarations, casts, etc., in exactly the same ways that the type `int` can be:

```
LENGTH    len, maxlen;
LENGTH    *lengths[];
```

Similarly, the declaration

```
typedef char *STRING;
```

makes `STRING` a synonym for `char *` or character pointer, which may then be used in declarations like

```
STRING p, lineptr[LINES], alloc();
```

Notice that the type being declared in a `typedef` appears in the position of a variable name, not right after the word `typedef`. Syntactically, `typedef` is like the storage classes `extern`, `static`, etc. We have also used upper case letters to emphasize the names.

As a more complicated example, we could make `typedef`'s for the tree nodes shown earlier in this chapter:

```
typedef struct tnode {         /* the basic node */
    char *word;      /* points to the text */
    int  count;      /* number of occurrences */
    struct tnode *left;      /* left child */
    struct tnode *right;      /* right child */
} TREENODE, *TREEPTR;
```

This creates two new type keywords called `TREENODE` (a structure) and `TREEPTR` (a pointer to the structure). Then the routine `talloc` could become

```
TREEPTR talloc()
{
    char *alloc();

    return((TREEPTR) alloc(sizeof(TREENODE)));
}
```

It must be emphasized that a `typedef` declaration does not create a new type in any sense; it merely adds a new name for some existing type. Nor are there any new semantics: variables declared this way have exactly the same properties as variables whose declarations are spelled out explicitly. In effect, `typedef` is like `#define`, except that since it is interpreted by the compiler, it can cope with textual substitutions that are beyond the capabilities of the C macro preprocessor. For example,

```
typedef int (*PFI)();
```

creates the type `PFI`, for "pointer to function returning `int`," which can be used in contexts like

```
PFI strcmp, numcmp, swap;
```

in the sort program of Chapter 5.

There are two main reasons for using `typedef` declarations. The first is to parameterize a program against portability problems. If `typedef`'s are used for data types which may be machine dependent, only the `typedef`'s need change when the program is moved. One common situation is to use `typedef` names for various integer quantities, then make an appropriate set of choices of `short`, `int` and `long` for each host machine.

The second purpose of `typedef`'s is to provide better documentation for a program — a type called `TREEPTR` may be easier to understand than one declared only as a pointer to a complicated structure.

Finally, there is always the possibility that in the future the compiler or some other program such as *lint* may make use of the information contained in `typedef` declarations to perform some extra checking of a program.

CHAPTER 7:   **INPUT AND OUTPUT**

Input and output facilities are not part of the C language, so we have de-emphasized them in our presentation thus far. Nonetheless, real programs do interact with their environment in much more complicated ways than those we have shown before. In this chapter we will describe "the standard I/O library," a set of functions designed to provide a standard I/O system for C programs. The functions are intended to present a convenient programming interface, yet reflect only operations that can be provided on most modern operating systems. The routines are efficient enough that users should seldom feel the need to circumvent them "for efficiency" regardless of how critical the application. Finally, the routines are meant to be "portable," in the sense that they will exist in compatible form on any system where C exists, and that programs which confine their system interactions to facilities provided by the standard library can be moved from one system to another essentially without change.

We will not try to describe the entire I/O library here; we are more interested in showing the essentials of writing C programs that interact with their operating system environment.

7.1   Access to the Standard Library

Each source file that refers to a standard library function must contain the line

```
#include <stdio.h>
```

near the beginning. The file `stdio.h` defines certain macros and variables used by the I/O library. Use of the angle brackets < and > instead of the usual double quotes directs the compiler to search for the file in a directory containing standard header information (on UNIX, typically *lusrlinclude*).

Furthermore, it may be necessary when loading the program to specify the library explicitly; for example, on the PDP-11 UNIX system, the command to compile a program would be

143

cc   *source files, etc.*   -lS

where -lS indicates loading from the standard library. (The character l is
the letter ell.)

7.2 Standard Input and Output — Getchar and Putchar

The simplest input mechanism is to read a character at a time from the
"standard input," generally the user's terminal, with `getchar`.
`getchar()` returns the next input character each time it is called. In most
environments that support C, a file may be substituted for the terminal by
using the < convention: if a program *prog* uses `getchar`, then the command line

```
prog <infile
```

causes *prog* to read `infile` instead of the terminal. The switching of the
input is done in such a way that *prog* itself is oblivious to the change; in particular, the string "`<infile`" is not included in the command-line arguments in `argv`. The input switching is also invisible if the input comes
from another program via a pipe mechanism; the command line

```
otherprog | prog
```

runs the two programs *otherprog* and *prog*, and arranges that the standard
input for *prog* comes from the standard output of *otherprog*.

`getchar` returns the value `EOF` when it encounters end of file on whatever input is being read. The standard library defines the symbolic constant
`EOF` to be -1 (with a `#define` in the file `stdio.h`), but tests should be
written in terms of `EOF`, not -1, so as to be independent of the specific
value.

For output, `putchar(c)` puts the character c on the "standard output," which is also by default the terminal. The output can be directed to a
file by using >: if *prog* uses `putchar`,

```
prog >outfile
```

will write the standard output onto `outfile` instead of the terminal. On
the UNIX system, a pipe can also be used:

```
prog | anotherprog
```

puts the standard output of *prog* into the standard input of *otherprog*. Again,
prog is not aware of the redirection.

Output produced by `printf` also finds its way to the standard output,
and calls to `putchar` and `printf` may be interleaved.

A surprising number of programs read only one input stream and write
only one output stream; for such programs I/O with `getchar`, `putchar`,
and `printf` may be entirely adequate, and is certainly enough to get

started. This is particularly true given file redirection and a pipe facility for connecting the output of one program to the input of the next. For example, consider the program *lower*, which maps its input to lower case:

```
#include   <stdio.h>

main()      /* convert input to lower case */
{
      int c;

      while ((c = getchar()) != EOF)
            putchar(isupper(c) ? tolower(c) : c);
}
```

The "functions" `isupper` and `tolower` are actually macros defined in `stdio.h`. The macro `isupper` tests whether its argument is an upper case letter, returning non-zero if it is, and zero if not. The macro `tolower` converts an upper case letter to lower case. Regardless of how these functions are implemented on a particular machine, their external behavior is the same, so programs that use them are shielded from knowledge of the character set.

To convert multiple files, you can use a program like the UNIX utility *cat* to collect the files:

```
cat file1 file2 ... | lower >output
```

and thus avoid learning how to access files from a program. (*cat* is presented later in this chapter.)

As an aside, in the standard I/O library the "functions" `getchar` and `putchar` can actually be macros, and thus avoid the overhead of a function call per character. We will show how this is done in Chapter 8.

7.3   Formatted Output — Printf

The two routines `printf` for output and `scanf` for input (next section) permit translation to and from character representations of numerical quantities. They also allow generation or interpretation of formatted lines. We have used `printf` informally throughout the previous chapters; here is a more complete and precise description.

```
printf(control, arg1, arg2, ...)
```

`printf` converts, formats, and prints its arguments on the standard output under control of the string `control`. The control string contains two types of objects: ordinary characters, which are simply copied to the output stream, and conversion specifications, each of which causes conversion and printing of the next successive argument to `printf`.

Each conversion specification is introduced by the character % and ended by a conversion character. Between the % and the conversion character there may be:

A minus sign, which specifies left adjustment of the converted argument in its field.

A digit string specifying a minimum field width. The converted number will be printed in a field at least this wide, and wider if necessary. If the converted argument has fewer characters than the field width it will be padded on the left (or right, if the left adjustment indicator has been given) to make up the field width. The padding character is blank normally and zero if the field width was specified with a leading zero (this zero does not imply an octal field width).

A period, which separates the field width from the next digit string.

A digit string (the precision), which specifies the maximum number of characters to be printed from a string, or the number of digits to be printed to the right of the decimal point of a float or double.

A length modifier l (letter ell), which indicates that the corresponding data item is a long rather than an int.

The conversion characters and their meanings are:

d   The argument is converted to decimal notation.

o   The argument is converted to unsigned octal notation (without a leading zero).

x   The argument is converted to unsigned hexadecimal notation (without a leading 0x).

u   The argument is converted to unsigned decimal notation.

c   The argument is taken to be a single character.

s   The argument is a string; characters from the string are printed until a null character is reached or until the number of characters indicated by the precision specification is exhausted.

e   The argument is taken to be a float or double and converted to decimal notation of the form [-]m.nnnnnnE[±]xx where the length of the string of n's is specified by the precision. The default precision is 6.

    f   The argument is taken to be a `float` or `double` and converted to decimal notation of the form `[-]mmm.nnnnn` where the length of the string of n's is specified by the precision. The default precision is 6. Note that the precision does not determine the number of significant digits printed in `f` format.

    g   Use `%e` or `%f`, whichever is shorter; non-significant zeros are not printed.

If the character after the `%` is not a conversion character, that character is printed; thus `%` may be printed by `%%`.

Most of the format conversions are obvious, and have been illustrated in earlier chapters. One exception is precision as it relates to strings. The following table shows the effect of a variety of specifications in printing "hello, world" (12 characters). We have put colons around each field so you can see its extent.

```
:%10s:      :hello, world:
:%-10s:     :hello, world:
:%20s:      :        hello, world:
:%-20s:     :hello, world       :
:%20.10s:   :          hello, wor:
:%-20.10s:  :hello, wor         :
:%.10s:     :hello, wor:
```

A warning: `printf` uses its first argument to decide how many arguments follow and what their types are. It will get confused, and you will get nonsense answers, if there are not enough arguments or if they are the wrong type.

Exercise 7-1. Write a program which will print arbitrary input in a sensible way. As a minimum, it should print non-graphic characters in octal or hex (according to local custom), and fold long lines. □

7.4 Formatted Input — Scanf

The function `scanf` is the input analog of `printf`, providing many of the same conversion facilities in the opposite direction.

```
scanf(control, arg1, arg2, ...)
```

`scanf` reads characters from the standard input, interprets them according to the format specified in `control`, and stores the results in the remaining arguments. The control argument is described below; the other arguments, *each of which must be a pointer,* indicate where the corresponding converted input should be stored.

The control string usually contains conversion specifications, which are used to direct interpretation of input sequences. The control string may contain:

Blanks, tabs or newlines ("white space characters"), which are ignored.

Ordinary characters (not %) which are expected to match the next non-white space character of the input stream.

Conversion specifications, consisting of the character %, an optional assignment suppression character *, an optional number specifying a maximum field width, and a conversion character.

A conversion specification directs the conversion of the next input field. Normally the result is placed in the variable pointed to by the corresponding argument. If assignment suppression is indicated by the * character, however, the input field is simply skipped; no assignment is made. An input field is defined as a string of non-white space characters; it extends either to the next white space character or until the field width, if specified, is exhausted. This implies that `scanf` will read across line boundaries to find its input, since newlines are white space.

The conversion character indicates the interpretation of the input field; the corresponding argument must be a pointer, as required by the call by value semantics of C. The following conversion characters are legal:

d   a decimal integer is expected in the input; the corresponding argument should be an integer pointer.

o   an octal integer (with or without a leading zero) is expected in the input; the corresponding argument should be a integer pointer.

x   a hexadecimal integer (with or without a leading `0x`) is expected in the input; the corresponding argument should be an integer pointer.

h   a `short` integer is expected in the input; the corresponding argument should be a pointer to a `short` integer.

c   a single character is expected; the corresponding argument should be a character pointer; the next input character is placed at the indicated spot. The normal skip over white space characters is suppressed in this case; to read the next non-white space character, use `%1s`.

> s   a character string is expected; the corresponding argu-
>   ment should be a character pointer pointing to an array
>   of characters large enough to accept the string and a
>   terminating \0 which will be added.
> f   a floating point number is expected; the corresponding
>   argument should be a pointer to a `float`. The conver-
>   sion character `e` is a synonym for `f`. The input format
>   for `float`'s is an optional sign, a string of numbers
>   possibly containing a decimal point, and an optional
>   exponent field containing an `E` or `e` followed by a possi-
>   bly signed integer.

The conversion characters d, o and x may be preceded by l (letter ell) to indicate that a pointer to `long` rather than `int` appears in the argument list. Similarly, the conversion characters e or f may be preceded by l to indicate that a pointer to `double` rather than `float` is in the argument list.

For example, the call

```
int  i;
float x;
char name[50];
scanf("%d %f %s", &i, &x, name);
```

with the input line

```
25    54.32E-1   Thompson
```

will assign the value 25 to i, the value 5.432 to x, and the string "Thompson", properly terminated by \0, to name. The three input fields may be separated by as many blanks, tabs and newlines as desired. The call

```
int  i;
float x;
char name[50];
scanf("%2d %f %*d %2s", &i, &x, name);
```

with input

```
56789 0123 45a72
```

will assign 56 to i, assign 789.0 to x, skip over 0123, and place the string "45" in name. The next call to any input routine will begin searching at the letter a. In these two examples, name *is* a pointer and thus must *not* be preceded by a &.

As another example, the rudimentary calculator of Chapter 4 can now be written with `scanf` to do the input conversion:

```
#include  <stdio.h>

main()    /* rudimentary desk calculator */
{
    double sum, v;

    sum = 0;
    while (scanf("%lf", &v) != EOF)
        printf("\t%.2f\n", sum += v);
}
```

scanf stops when it exhausts its control string, or when some input
fails to match the control specification. It returns as its value the number of
successfully matched and assigned input items. This can be used to decide
how many input items were found. On end of file, EOF is returned; note
that this is different from 0, which means that the next input character does
not match the first specification in the control string. The next call to
scanf resumes searching immediately after the last character already
returned.

A final warning: the arguments to scanf *must* be pointers. By far the
most common error is writing

```
scanf("%d", n);
```

instead of

```
scanf("%d", &n);
```

7.5 In-memory Format Conversion

The functions scanf and printf have siblings called sscanf and
sprintf which perform the corresponding conversions, but operate on a
string instead of a file. The general format is

```
sprintf(string, control, arg1, arg2, ...)
sscanf(string, control, arg1, arg2, ...)
```

sprintf formats the arguments in arg1, arg2, etc., according to
control as before, but places the result in string instead of on the standard output. Of course string had better be big enough to receive the
result. As an example, if name is a character array and n is an integer, then

```
sprintf(name, "temp%d", n);
```

creates a string of the form temp*nnn* in name, where *nnn* is the value of
n.

sscanf does the reverse conversions — it scans the string according
to the format in control, and places the resulting values in arg1, arg2,
etc. These arguments must be pointers. The call

```
    sscanf(name, "temp%d", &n);
```

sets n to the value of the string of digits following temp in name.

Exercise 7-2. Rewrite the desk calculator of Chapter 4 using scanf and/or sscanf to do the input and number conversion. □

7.6   File Access

The programs written so far have all read the standard input and written the standard output, which we have assumed are magically pre-defined for a program by the local operating system.

The next step in I/O is to write a program that accesses a file which is *not* already connected to the program. One program that clearly illustrates the need for such operations is *cat*, which concatenates a set of named files onto the standard output. *cat* is used for printing files on the terminal, and as a general-purpose input collector for programs which do not have the capability of accessing files by name. For example, the command

```
    cat x.c y.c
```

prints the contents of the files x.c and y.c on the standard output.

The question is how to arrange for the named files to be read — that is, how to connect the external names that a user thinks of to the statements which actually read the data.

The rules are simple. Before it can be read or written a file has to be *opened* by the standard library function fopen. fopen takes an external name (like x.c or y.c), does some housekeeping and negotiation with the operating system (details of which needn't concern us), and returns an internal name which must be used in subsequent reads or write of the file.

This internal name is actually a pointer, called a *file pointer*, to a structure which contains information about the file, such as the location of a buffer, the current character position in the buffer, whether the file is being read or written, and the like. Users don't need to know the details, because part of the standard I/O definitions obtained from stdio.h is a structure definition called FILE. The only declaration needed for a file pointer is exemplified by

```
    FILE *fopen(), *fp;
```

This says that fp is a pointer to a FILE, and fopen returns a pointer to a FILE. Notice that FILE is a type name, like int, not a structure tag; it is implemented as a typedef. (Details of how this all works on the UNIX system are given in Chapter 8.)

The actual call to fopen in a program is

```
    fp = fopen(name, mode);
```

The first argument of `fopen` is the *name* of the file, as a character string. The second argument is the *mode*, also as a character string, which indicates how one intends to use the file. Allowable modes are read (`"r"`), write (`"w"`), or append (`"a"`).

If you open a file which does not exist for writing or appending, it is created (if possible). Opening an existing file for writing causes the old contents to be discarded. Trying to read a file that does not exist is an error, and there may be other causes of error as well (like trying to read a file when you don't have permission). If there is any error, `fopen` will return the null pointer value `NULL` (which for convenience is also defined in `stdio.h`).

The next thing needed is a way to read or write the file once it is open. There are several possibilities, of which `getc` and `putc` are the simplest. `getc` returns the next character from a file; it needs the file pointer to tell it what file. Thus

```
c = getc(fp)
```

places in `c` the next character from the file referred to by `fp`, and `EOF` when it reaches end of file.

`putc` is the inverse of `getc`:

```
putc(c, fp)
```

puts the character `c` on the file `fp` and returns `c`. Like `getchar` and `putchar`, `getc` and `putc` may be macros instead of functions.

When a program is started, three files are opened automatically, and file pointers are provided for them. These files are the standard input, the standard output, and the standard error output; the corresponding file pointers are called `stdin`, `stdout`, and `stderr`. Normally these are all connected to the terminal, but `stdin` and `stdout` may be redirected to files or pipes as described in section 7.2.

`getchar` and `putchar` can be defined in terms of `getc`, `putc`, `stdin` and `stdout` as follows:

```
#define getchar()   getc(stdin)
#define putchar(c)  putc(c, stdout)
```

For formatted input or output of files, the functions `fscanf` and `fprintf` may be used. These are identical to `scanf` and `printf`, save that the first argument is a file pointer that specifies the file to be read or written; the control string is the second argument.

With these preliminaries out of the way, we are now in a position to write the program *cat* to concatenate files. The basic design is one that has been found convenient for many programs: if there are command-line arguments, they are processed in order. If there are no arguments, the standard

input is processed. This way the program can be used stand-alone or as part
of a larger process.

```
#include   <stdio.h>

main(argc, argv)      /* cat: concatenate files */
int argc;
char *argv[];
{
     FILE *fp, *fopen();

     if (argc == 1) /* no args; copy standard input */
         filecopy(stdin);
     else
         while (--argc > 0)
              if ((fp = fopen(*++argv, "r")) == NULL) {
                   printf("cat: can't open %s\n", *argv);
                   break;
              } else {
                   filecopy(fp);
                   fclose(fp);
              }
}

filecopy(fp)     /* copy file fp to standard output */
FILE *fp;
{
     int c;

     while ((c = getc(fp)) != EOF)
          putc(c, stdout);
}
```

The file pointers stdin and stdout are pre-defined in the I/O library as
the standard input and standard output; they may be used anywhere an
object of type FILE * can be. They are constants, however, *not* variables,
so don't try to assign to them.

The function fclose is the inverse of fopen; it breaks the connection
between the file pointer and the external name that was established by
fopen, freeing the file pointer for another file. Since most operating systems have some limit on the number of simultaneously open files that a
program may have, it's a good idea to free things when they are no longer
needed, as we did in *cat*. There is also another reason for fclose on an
output file — it flushes the buffer in which putc is collecting output.
(fclose is called automatically for each open file when a program terminates normally.)

7.7   Error Handling — Stderr and Exit

The treatment of errors in *cat* is not ideal. The trouble is that if one of the files can't be accessed for some reason, the diagnostic is printed at the end of the concatenated output. That is acceptable if that output is going to a terminal, but bad if it's going into a file or into another program via a pipeline.

To handle this situation better, a second output file, called `stderr`, is assigned to a program in the same way that `stdin` and `stdout` are. If at all possible, output written on `stderr` appears on the user's terminal even if the standard output is redirected.

Let us revise *cat* to write its error messages on the standard error file.

```
#include  <stdio.h>

main(argc, argv)     /* cat: concatenate files */
int argc;
char *argv[];
{
     FILE *fp, *fopen();

     if (argc == 1) /* no args; copy standard input */
          filecopy(stdin);
     else
          while (--argc > 0)
               if ((fp = fopen(*++argv, "r")) == NULL) {
                    fprintf(stderr,
                         "cat: can't open %s\n", *argv);
                    exit(1);
               } else {
                    filecopy(fp);
                    fclose(fp);
               }
     exit(0);
}
```

The program signals errors two ways. The diagnostic output produced by `fprintf` goes onto `stderr`, so it finds its way to the user's terminal instead of disappearing down a pipeline or into an output file.

The program also uses the standard library function `exit`, which terminates program execution when it is called. The argument of `exit` is available to whatever process called this one, so the success or failure of the program can be tested by another program that uses this one as a subprocess. By convention, a return value of 0 signals that all is well, and various non-zero values signal abnormal situations.

`exit` calls `fclose` for each open output file, to flush out any buffered output, then calls a routine named `_exit`. The function `_exit` causes immediate termination without any buffer flushing; of course it may be called directly if desired.

7.8   Line Input and Output

The standard library provides a routine `fgets` which is quite similar to the `getline` function that we have used throughout the book. The call

        fgets(line, MAXLINE, fp)

reads the next input line (including the newline) from file `fp` into the character array `line`; at most `MAXLINE-1` characters will be read. The resulting line is terminated with `\0`. Normally `fgets` returns `line`; on end of file it returns `NULL`. (Our `getline` returns the line length, and zero for end of file.)

For output, the function `fputs` writes a string (which need not contain a newline) to a file:

        fputs(line, fp)

To show that there is nothing magic about functions like `fgets` and `fputs`, here they are, copied directly from the standard I/O library:

```
#include   <stdio.h>

char *fgets(s, n, iop)   /* get at most n chars from iop */
char *s;
int n;
register FILE *iop;
{
     register int c;
     register char *cs;

     cs = s;
     while (--n > 0 && (c = getc(iop)) != EOF)
          if ((*cs++ = c) == '\n')
               break;
     *cs = '\0';
     return((c == EOF && cs == s) ? NULL : s);
}
```

```
fputs(s, iop)  /* put string s on file iop */
register char *s;
register FILE *iop;
{
      register int c;

      while (c = *s++)
           putc(c, iop);
}
```

Exercise 7-3. Write a program to compare two files, printing the first line and character position where they differ. □

Exercise 7-4. Modify the pattern finding program of Chapter 5 to take its input from a set of named files or, if no files are named as arguments, from the standard input. Should the file name be printed when a matching line is found? □

Exercise 7-5. Write a program to print a set of files, starting each new one on a new page, with a title and a running page count for each file. □

7.9   Some Miscellaneous Functions

The standard library provides a variety of functions, a few of which stand out as especially useful. We have already mentioned the string functions `strlen`, `strcpy`, `strcat` and `strcmp`. Here are some others.

Character Class Testing and Conversion

Several macros perform character tests and conversions:

`isalpha(c)`	non-zero if c is alphabetic, 0 if not.
`isupper(c)`	non-zero if c is upper case, 0 if not.
`islower(c)`	non-zero if c is lower case, 0 if not.
`isdigit(c)`	non-zero if c is digit, 0 if not.
`isspace(c)`	non-zero if c is blank, tab or newline, 0 if not.
`toupper(c)`	convert c to upper case.
`tolower(c)`	convert c to lower case.

Ungetc

The standard library provides a rather restricted version of the function `ungetch` which we wrote in Chapter 4; it is called `ungetc`.

```
ungetc(c, fp)
```

pushes the character c back onto file `fp`. Only one character of pushback is allowed per file. `ungetc` may be used with any of the input functions and macros like `scanf`, `getc`, or `getchar`.

System Call

The function `system(s)` executes the command contained in the character string `s`, then resumes execution of the current program. The contents of `s` depend strongly on the local operating system. As a trivial example, on UNIX, the line

```
system("date");
```

causes the program `date` to be run; it prints the date and time of day.

Storage Management

The function `calloc` is rather like the `alloc` we have used in previous chapters.

```
calloc(n, sizeof(object))
```

returns a pointer to enough space for `n` objects of the specified size, or `NULL` if the request cannot be satisfied. The storage is initialized to zero.

The pointer has the proper alignment for the object in question, but it should be cast into the appropriate type, as in

```
char *calloc();
int  *ip;

ip = (int *) calloc(n, sizeof(int));
```

`cfree(p)` frees the space pointed to by `p`, where `p` is originally obtained by a call to `calloc`. There are no restrictions on the order in which space is freed, but it is a ghastly error to free something not obtained by calling `calloc`.

Chapter 8 shows the implementation of a storage allocator like `calloc`, in which allocated blocks may be freed in any order.

CHAPTER 8:   **THE UNIX SYSTEM INTERFACE**

The material in this chapter is concerned with the interface between C programs and the UNIX† operating system. Since most C users are on UNIX systems, this should be helpful to a majority of readers. Even if you use C on a different machine, however, you should be able to glean more insight into C programming from studying these examples.

The chapter is divided into three major areas: input/output, file system, and a storage allocator. The first two parts assume a modest familiarity with the external characteristics of UNIX.

Chapter 7 was concerned with a system interface that is uniform across a variety of operating systems. On any particular system the routines of the standard library have to be written in terms of the I/O facilities actually available on the host system. In the next few sections we will describe the basic system entry points for I/O on the UNIX operating system, and illustrate how parts of the standard library can be implemented with them.

8.1 File Descriptors

In the UNIX operating system, all input and output is done by reading or writing files, because all peripheral devices, even the user's terminal, are files in the file system. This means that a single, homogeneous interface handles all communication between a program and peripheral devices.

In the most general case, before reading or writing a file, it is necessary to inform the system of your intent to do so, a process called "opening" the file. If you are going to write on a file it may also be necessary to create it. The system checks your right to do so (Does the file exist? Do you have permission to access it?), and if all is well, returns to the program a small positive integer called a *file descriptor*. Whenever I/O is to be done on the file, the file descriptor is used instead of the name to identify the file. (This is roughly analogous to the use of READ(5,...) and WRITE(6,...) in Fortran.) All information about an open file is maintained by the system; the user

---

† UNIX is a Trademark of Bell Laboratories.

program refers to the file only by the file descriptor.

Since input and output involving the user's terminal is so common, special arrangements exist to make this convenient. When the command interpreter (the "shell") runs a program, it opens three files, with file descriptors 0, 1, and 2, called the standard input, the standard output, and the standard error output. All of these are normally connected to the terminal, so if a program reads file descriptor 0 and writes file descriptors 1 and 2, it can do terminal I/O without worrying about opening the files.

The user of a program can *redirect* I/O to and from files with < and >:

```
prog <infile >outfile
```

In this case, the shell changes the default assignments for file descriptors 0 and 1 from the terminal to the named files. Normally file descriptor 2 remains attached to the terminal, so error messages can go there. Similar observations hold if the input or output is associated with a pipe. In all cases, it must be noted, the file assignments are changed by the shell, not by the program. The program does not know where its input comes from nor where its output goes, so long as it uses file 0 for input and 1 and 2 for output.

8.2   Low Level I/O — Read and Write

The lowest level of I/O in UNIX provides no buffering or any other services; it is in fact a direct entry into the operating system. All input and output is done by two functions called `read` and `write`. For both, the first argument is a file descriptor. The second argument is a buffer in your program where the data is to come from or go to. The third argument is the number of bytes to be transferred. The calls are

```
n_read = read(fd, buf, n);

n_written = write(fd, buf, n);
```

Each call returns a byte count which is the number of bytes actually transferred. On reading, the number of bytes returned may be less than the number asked for. A return value of zero bytes implies end of file, and −1 indicates an error of some sort. For writing, the returned value is the number of bytes actually written; it is generally an error if this isn't equal to the number supposed to be written.

The number of bytes to be read or written is quite arbitrary. The two most common values are 1, which means one character at a time ("unbuffered"), and 512, which corresponds to a physical blocksize on many peripheral devices. This latter size will be most efficient, but even character at a time I/O is not inordinately expensive.

Putting these facts together, we can write a simple program to copy its input to its output, the equivalent of the file copying program written for Chapter 1. In UNIX, this program will copy anything to anything, since the input and output can be redirected to any file or device.

```
#define   BUFSIZE   512  /* best size for PDP-11 UNIX */

main()     /* copy input to output */
{
      char buf[BUFSIZE];
      int  n;

      while ((n = read(0, buf, BUFSIZE)) > 0)
            write(1, buf, n);
}
```

If the file size is not a multiple of BUFSIZE, some read will return a smaller number of bytes to be written by write; the next call to read after that will return zero.

It is instructive to see how read and write can be used to construct higher level routines like getchar, putchar, etc. For example, here is a version of getchar which does unbuffered input.

```
#define   CMASK        0377 /* for making char's > 0 */

getchar() /* unbuffered single character input */
{
      char c;

      return((read(0, &c, 1) > 0) ? c & CMASK : EOF);
}
```

c *must* be declared char, because read accepts a character pointer. The character being returned must be masked with 0377 to ensure that it is positive; otherwise sign extension may make it negative. (The constant 0377 is appropriate for the PDP-11 but not necessarily for other machines.)

The second version of getchar does input in big chunks, and hands out the characters one at a time.

```
#define    CMASK      0377 /* for making char's > 0 */
#define    BUFSIZE    512

getchar() /* buffered version */
{
     static char    buf[BUFSIZE];
     static char    *bufp = buf;
     static int     n = 0;

     if (n == 0) {  /* buffer is empty */
          n = read(0, buf, BUFSIZE);
          bufp = buf;
     }
     return((--n >= 0) ? *bufp++ & CMASK : EOF);
}
```

8.3   Open, Creat, Close, Unlink

Other than the default standard input, output and error files, you must explicitly open files in order to read or write them. There are two system entry points for this, open and creat [sic].

open is rather like the fopen discussed in Chapter 7, except that instead of returning a file pointer, it returns a file descriptor, which is just an int.

```
int fd;

fd = open(name, rwmode);
```

As with fopen, the name argument is a character string corresponding to the external file name. The access mode argument is different, however: rwmode is 0 for read, 1 for write, and 2 for read and write access. open returns −1 if any error occurs; otherwise it returns a valid file descriptor.

It is an error to try to open a file that does not exist. The entry point creat is provided to create new files, or to re-write old ones.

```
fd = creat(name, pmode);
```

returns a file descriptor if it was able to create the file called name, and −1 if not. If the file already exists, creat will truncate it to zero length; it is not an error to creat a file that already exists.

If the file is brand new, creat creates it with the *protection mode* specified by the pmode argument. In the UNIX file system, there are nine bits of protection information associated with a file, controlling read, write and execute permission for the owner of the file, for the owner's group, and for all others. Thus a three-digit octal number is most convenient for specifying the permissions. For example, 0755 specifies read, write and execute permission for the owner, and read and execute permission for the group and everyone else.

To illustrate, here is a simplified version of the UNIX utility *cp*, a program which copies one file to another. (The main simplification is that our version copies only one file, and does not permit the second argument to be a directory.)

```
#define NULL 0
#define BUFSIZE 512
#define PMODE 0644 /* RW for owner, R for group, others */

main(argc, argv)     /* cp: copy f1 to f2 */
int argc;
char *argv[];
{
    int  f1, f2, n;
    char buf[BUFSIZE];

    if (argc != 3)
        error("Usage: cp from to", NULL);
    if ((f1 = open(argv[1], 0)) == -1)
        error("cp: can't open %s", argv[1]);
    if ((f2 = creat(argv[2], PMODE)) == -1)
        error("cp: can't create %s", argv[2]);

    while ((n = read(f1, buf, BUFSIZE)) > 0)
        if (write(f2, buf, n) != n)
            error("cp: write error", NULL);
    exit(0);
}

error(s1, s2)  /* print error message and die */
char *s1, *s2;
{
    printf(s1, s2);
    printf("\n");
    exit(1);
}
```

There is a limit (typically 15-25) on the number of files which a program may have open simultaneously. Accordingly, any program which intends to process many files must be prepared to re-use file descriptors. The routine `close` breaks the connection between a file descriptor and an open file, and frees the file descriptor for use with some other file. Termination of a program via `exit` or return from the main program closes all open files.

The function `unlink(filename)` removes the file `filename` from the file system.

Exercise 8-1. Rewrite the program `cat` from Chapter 7 using `read`, `write`, `open` and `close` instead of their standard library equivalents. Perform experiments to determine the relative speeds of the two versions. □

8.4 Random Access — Seek and Lseek

File I/O is normally sequential: each `read` or `write` takes place at a position in the file right after the previous one. When necessary, however, a file can be read or written in any arbitrary order. The system call `lseek` provides a way to move around in a file without actually reading or writing:

```
lseek(fd, offset, origin);
```

forces the current position in the file whose descriptor is `fd` to move to position `offset`, which is taken relative to the location specified by `origin`. Subsequent reading or writing will begin at that position. `offset` is a `long`; `fd` and `origin` are `int`'s. `origin` can be 0, 1, or 2 to specify that `offset` is to be measured from the beginning, from the current position, or from the end of the file respectively. For example, to append to a file, seek to the end before writing:

```
lseek(fd, 0L, 2);
```

To get back to the beginning ("rewind"),

```
lseek(fd, 0L, 0);
```

Notice the `0L` argument; it could also be written as `(long) 0`.

With `lseek`, it is possible to treat files more or less like large arrays, at the price of slower access. For example, the following simple function reads any number of bytes from any arbitrary place in a file.

```
get(fd, pos, buf, n)  /* read n bytes from position pos */
int fd, n;
long pos;
char *buf;
{
    lseek(fd, pos, 0);   /* get to pos */
    return(read(fd, buf, n));
}
```

In pre-version 7 UNIX, the basic entry point to the I/O system is called `seek`. `seek` is identical to `lseek`, except that its `offset` argument is an `int` rather than a `long`. Accordingly, since PDP-11 integers have only 16 bits, the `offset` specified for `seek` is limited to 65,535; for this reason, `origin` values of 3, 4, 5 cause `seek` to multiply the given offset by 512 (the number of bytes in one physical block) and then interpret `origin` as if it were 0, 1, or 2 respectively. Thus to get to an arbitrary place in a large file requires two seeks, first one which selects the block, then one which has origin equal to 1 and moves to the desired byte within the block.

Exercise 8-2. Clearly, seek can be written in terms of lseek, and vice versa. Write each in terms of the other. □

8.5   Example — An Implementation of Fopen and Getc

Let us illustrate how some of these pieces fit together by showing an implementation of the standard library routines fopen and getc.

Recall that files in the standard library are described by file pointers rather than file descriptors. A file pointer is a pointer to a structure that contains several pieces of information about the file: a pointer to a buffer, so the file can be read in large chunks; a count of the number of characters left in the buffer; a pointer to the next character position in the buffer; some flags describing read/write mode, etc.; and the file descriptor.

The data structure that describes a file is contained in the file stdio.h, which must be included (by #include) in any source file that uses routines from the standard library. It is also included by functions in that library. In the following excerpt from stdio.h, names which are intended for use only by functions of the library begin with an underscore so they are less likely to collide with names in a user's program.

```
#define    _BUFSIZE   512
#define    _NFILE     20    /* #files that can be handled */

typedef struct _iobuf {
      char *_ptr;      /* next character position */
      int  _cnt;       /* number of characters left */
      char *_base;     /* location of buffer */
      int  _flag;      /* mode of file access */
      int  _fd;        /* file descriptor */
} FILE;
extern FILE _iob[_NFILE];

#define    stdin      (&_iob[0])
#define    stdout     (&_iob[1])
#define    stderr     (&_iob[2])

#define    _READ      01    /* file open for reading */
#define    _WRITE     02    /* file open for writing */
#define    _UNBUF     04    /* file is unbuffered */
#define    _BIGBUF    010   /* big buffer allocated */
#define    _EOF 020         /* EOF has occurred on this file */
#define    _ERR 040         /* error has occurred on this file */
#define    NULL 0
#define    EOF  (-1)
```

```
#define    getc(p)    (--(p)->_cnt >= 0 \
                    ? *(p)->_ptr++ & 0377 : _fillbuf(p))
#define    getchar() getc(stdin)

#define    putc(x,p)  (--(p)->_cnt >= 0 \
                    ? *(p)->_ptr++ = (x) : _flushbuf((x),p))
#define    putchar(x)     putc(x,stdout)
```

The getc macro normally just decrements the count, advances the pointer, and returns the character. (A long #define is continued with a backslash.) If the count goes negative, however, getc calls the function _fillbuf to replenish the buffer, re-initialize the structure contents, and return a character. A function may present a portable interface, yet itself contain non-portable constructs: getc masks the character with 0377, which defeats the sign extension done by the PDP-11 and ensures that all characters will be positive.

Although we will not discuss any details, we have included the definition of putc to show that it operates in much the same way as getc, calling a function _flushbuf when its buffer is full.

The function fopen can now be written. Most of fopen is concerned with getting the file opened and positioned at the right place, and setting the flag bits to indicate the proper state. fopen does not allocate any buffer space; this is done by _fillbuf when the file is first read.

```
#include  <stdio.h>
#define   PMODE      0644 /* R/W for owner; R for others */

FILE *fopen(name, mode)   /* open file, return file ptr */
register char *name, *mode;
{
    register int fd;
    register FILE *fp;

    if (*mode != 'r' && *mode != 'w' && *mode != 'a') {
        fprintf(stderr, "illegal mode %s opening %s\n",
            mode, name);
        exit(1);
    }
    for (fp = _iob; fp < _iob + _NFILE; fp++)
        if ((fp->_flag & (_READ | _WRITE)) == 0)
            break;     /* found free slot */
    if (fp >= _iob + _NFILE) /* no free slots */
        return(NULL);

    if (*mode == 'w')   /* access file */
        fd = creat(name, PMODE);
    else if (*mode == 'a') {
        if ((fd = open(name, 1)) == -1)
            fd = creat(name, PMODE);
        lseek(fd, 0L, 2);
    } else
        fd = open(name, 0);
    if (fd == -1)   /* couldn't access name */
        return(NULL);

    fp->_fd = fd;
    fp->_cnt = 0;
    fp->_base = NULL;
    fp->_flag &= ~(_READ | _WRITE);
    fp->_flag |= (*mode == 'r') ? _READ : _WRITE;
    return(fp);
}
```

The function _fillbuf is rather more complicated. The main complexity lies in the fact that _fillbuf attempts to permit access to the file even though there may not be enough memory to buffer the I/O. If space for a new buffer can be obtained from calloc, all is well; if not, _fillbuf does unbuffered I/O using a single character stored in a private array.

```
#include  <stdio.h>

_fillbuf(fp)  /* allocate and fill input buffer */
register FILE *fp;
{
    static char smallbuf[_NFILE]; /* for unbuffered I/O */
    char *calloc();

    if ((fp->_flag&_READ)==0 || (fp->_flag&(_EOF|_ERR))!=0)
        return(EOF);
    while (fp->_base == NULL)  /* find buffer space */
        if (fp->_flag & _UNBUF)  /* unbuffered */
            fp->_base = &smallbuf[fp->_fd];
        else if ((fp->_base=calloc(_BUFSIZE, 1)) == NULL)
            fp->_flag |= _UNBUF; /* can't get big buf */
        else
            fp->_flag |= _BIGBUF; /* got big one */
    fp->_ptr = fp->_base;
    fp->_cnt = read(fp->_fd, fp->_ptr,
                    fp->_flag & _UNBUF ? 1 : _BUFSIZE);
    if (--fp->_cnt < 0) {
        if (fp->_cnt == -1)
            fp->_flag |= _EOF;
        else
            fp->_flag |= _ERR;
        fp->_cnt = 0;
        return(EOF);
    }
    return(*fp->_ptr++ & 0377);   /* make char positive */
}
```

The first call to getc for a particular file finds a count of zero, which forces
a call of _fillbuf. If _fillbuf finds that the file is not open for reading, it returns EOF immediately. Otherwise, it tries to allocate a large
buffer, and, failing that, a single character buffer, setting the buffering information in _flag appropriately.

Once the buffer is established, _fillbuf simply calls read to fill it,
sets the count and pointers, and returns the character at the beginning of
the buffer. Subsequent calls to _fillbuf will find a buffer allocated.

The only remaining loose end is how everything gets started. The array
_iob must be defined and initialized for stdin, stdout and stderr:

```
FILE _iob[_NFILE] ={
    { NULL, 0, NULL, _READ, 0 },  /* stdin */
    { NULL, 0, NULL, _WRITE, 1 }, /* stdout */
    { NULL, 0, NULL, _WRITE | _UNBUF, 2 }   /* stderr */
};
```

The initialization of the _flag part of the structure shows that stdin is to be read, stdout is to be written, and stderr is to be written unbuffered.

Exercise 8-3. Rewrite fopen and _fillbuf with fields instead of explicit bit operations. □

Exercise 8-4. Design and write the routines _flushbuf and fclose. □

Exercise 8-5. The standard library provides a function

```
fseek(fp, offset, origin)
```

which is identical to lseek except that fp is a file pointer instead of a file descriptor. Write fseek. Make sure that your fseek coordinates properly with the buffering done for the other functions of the library. □

8.6 Example — Listing Directories

A different kind of file system interaction is sometimes called for — determining information *about* a file, not what it contains. The UNIX command *ls* ("list directory") is an example — it prints the names of files in a directory, and optionally, other information, such as sizes, permissions, and so on.

Since on UNIX at least a directory is just a file, there is nothing special about a command like *ls*; it reads a file and picks out the relevant parts of the information it finds there. Nonetheless, the format of that information is determined by the system, not by a user program, so *ls* needs to know how the system represents things.

We will illustrate some of this by writing a program called *fsize*. *fsize* is a special form of *ls* which prints the sizes of all files named in its argument list. If one of the files is a directory, *fsize* applies itself recursively to that directory. If there are no arguments at all, it processes the current directory.

To begin, a short review of file system structure. A directory is a file that contains a list of file names and some indication of where they are located. The "location" is actually an index into another table called the "inode table." The inode for a file is where all information about a file except its name is kept. A directory entry consists of only two items, an inode number and the file name. The precise specification comes by including the file sys/dir.h, which contains

```
#define    DIRSIZ    14    /* max length of file name */

struct direct    /* structure of directory entry */
{
      ino_t d_ino;    /* inode number */
      char d_name[DIRSIZ];    /* file name */
};
```

The "type" `ino_t` is a `typedef` describing the index into the inode table. It happens to be `unsigned` on PDP-11 UNIX, but this is not the sort of information to embed in a program: it might be different on a different system. Hence the `typedef`. A complete set of "system" types is found in `sys/types.h`.

The function `stat` takes a file name and returns all of the information in the inode for that file (or −1 if there is an error). That is,

```
struct stat stbuf;
char *name;

stat(name, &stbuf);
```

fills the structure `stbuf` with the inode information for the file `name`. The structure describing the value returned by `stat` is in `sys/stat.h`, and looks like this:

```
struct stat      /* structure returned by stat */
{
      dev_t    st_dev;    /* device of inode */
      ino_t    st_ino;    /* inode number */
      short    st_mode;   /* mode bits */
      short    st_nlink;  /* number of links to file */
      short    st_uid;    /* owner's userid */
      short    st_gid;    /* owner's group id */
      dev_t    st_rdev;   /* for special files */
      off_t    st_size;   /* file size in characters */
      time_t   st_atime;  /* time last accessed */
      time_t   st_mtime;  /* time last modified */
      time_t   st_ctime;  /* time originally created */
};
```

Most of these are explained by the comment fields. The `st_mode` entry contains a set of flags describing the file; for convenience, the flag definitions are also part of the file `sys/stat.h`.

```
#define S_IFMT 0160000         /* type of file */
#define    S_IFDIR   0040000   /* directory */
#define    S_IFCHR   0020000   /* character special */
#define    S_IFBLK   0060000   /* block special */
#define    S_IFREG   0100000   /* regular */
#define S_ISUID      04000  /* set user id on execution */
#define S_ISGID      02000  /* set group id on execution */
#define S_ISVTX      01000  /* save swapped text after use */
#define S_IREAD      0400   /* read permission */
#define S_IWRITE     0200   /* write permission */
#define S_IEXEC      0100   /* execute permission */
```

Now we are able to write the program *fsize*. If the mode obtained from stat indicates that a file is not a directory, then the size is at hand and can be printed directly. If it is a directory, however, then we have to process that directory one file at a time; it in turn may contain sub-directories, so the process is recursive.

The main routine as usual deals primarily with command-line arguments; it hands each argument to the function fsize in a big buffer.

```
#include <stdio.h>
#include <sys/types.h>    /* typedefs */
#include <sys/dir.h>      /* directory entry structure */
#include <sys/stat.h>     /* structure returned by stat */
#define    BUFSIZE    256

main(argc, argv)    /* fsize: print file sizes */
char *argv[];
{
      char buf[BUFSIZE];

      if (argc == 1) {    /* default: current directory */
            strcpy(buf, ".");
            fsize(buf);
      } else
            while (--argc > 0) {
                  strcpy(buf, *++argv);
                  fsize(buf);
            }
}
```

The function fsize prints the size of the file. If the file is a directory, however, fsize first calls directory to handle all the files in it. Note the use of the flag names S_IFMT and S_IFDIR from stat.h.

```
fsize(name)      /* print size for name */
char *name;
{
    struct stat stbuf;

    if (stat(name, &stbuf) == -1) {
        fprintf(stderr, "fsize: can't find %s\n", name);
        return;
    }
    if ((stbuf.st_mode & S_IFMT) == S_IFDIR)
        directory(name);
    printf("%8ld %s\n", stbuf.st_size, name);
}
```

The function `directory` is the most complicated. Much of it is concerned, however, with creating the full pathname of the file being dealt with.

```
directory(name)      /* fsize for all files in name */
char *name;
{
    struct direct dirbuf;
    char *nbp, *nep;
    int i, fd;

    nbp = name + strlen(name);
    *nbp++ = '/';   /* add slash to directory name */
    if (nbp+DIRSIZ+2 >= name+BUFSIZE)   /* name too long */
        return;
    if ((fd = open(name, 0)) == -1)
        return;
    while (read(fd, (char *)&dirbuf, sizeof(dirbuf))>0) {
        if (dirbuf.d_ino == 0)   /* slot not in use */
            continue;
        if (strcmp(dirbuf.d_name, ".") == 0
          || strcmp(dirbuf.d_name, "..") == 0)
            continue; /* skip self and parent */
        for (i=0, nep=nbp; i < DIRSIZ; i++)
            *nep++ = dirbuf.d_name[i];
        *nep++ = '\0';
        fsize(name);
    }
    close(fd);
    *--nbp = '\0'; /* restore name */
}
```

If a directory slot is not currently in use (because a file has been removed), the inode entry is zero, and this position is skipped. Each directory also contains entries for itself, called " . ", and its parent, " . . "; clearly these must also be skipped, or the program will run for quite a while.

Although the *fsize* program is rather specialized, it does indicate a couple of important ideas. First, many programs are not "system programs"; they merely use information whose form or content is maintained by the operating system. Second, for such programs, it is crucial that the representation of the information appear only in standard "header files" like `stat.h` and `dir.h`, and that programs include those files instead of embedding the actual declarations in themselves.

8.7 Example — A Storage Allocator

In Chapter 5, we presented a simple-minded version of `alloc`. The version which we will now write is unrestricted: calls to `alloc` and `free` may be intermixed in any order; `alloc` calls upon the operating system to obtain more memory as necessary. Besides being useful in their own right, these routines illustrate some of the considerations involved in writing machine-dependent code in a relatively machine-independent way, and also show a real-life application of structures, unions and `typedef`.

Rather than allocating from a compiled-in fixed-sized array, `alloc` will request space from the operating system as needed. Since other activities in the program may also request space asynchronously, the space `alloc` manages may not be contiguous. Thus its free storage is kept as a chain of free blocks. Each block contains a size, a pointer to the next block, and the space itself. The blocks are kept in order of increasing storage address, and the last block (highest address) points to the first, so the chain is actually a ring.

When a request is made, the free list is scanned until a big enough block is found. If the block is exactly the size requested it is unlinked from the list and returned to the user. If the block is too big, it is split, and the proper amount is returned to the user while the residue is put back on the free list. If no big enough block is found, another block is obtained from the operating system and linked into the free list; searching then resumes.

Freeing also causes a search of the free list, to find the proper place to insert the block being freed. If the block being freed is adjacent to a free list block on either side, it is coalesced with it into a single bigger block, so storage does not become too fragmented. Determining adjacency is easy because the free list is maintained in storage order.

One problem, which we alluded to in Chapter 5, is to ensure that the storage returned by `alloc` is aligned properly for the objects that will be stored in it. Although machines vary, for each machine there is a most restrictive type: if the most restricted type can be stored at a particular address, all other types may be also. For example, on the IBM 360/370, the Honeywell 6000, and many other machines, any object may be stored on a boundary appropriate for a `double`; on the PDP-11, `int` suffices.

A free block contains a pointer to the next block in the chain, a record of the size of the block, and then the free space itself; the control information at the beginning is called the "header." To simplify alignment, all blocks are multiples of the header size, and the header is aligned properly. This is achieved by a union that contains the desired header structure and an instance of the most restrictive alignment type:

```
typedef int ALIGN;   /* forces alignment on PDP-11 */

union header { /* free block header */
    struct {
        union header *ptr;   /* next free block */
        unsigned size; /* size of this free block */
    } s;
    ALIGN      x;   /* force alignment of blocks */
};

typedef union header HEADER;
```

In `alloc`, the requested size in characters is rounded up to the proper number of header-sized units; the actual block that will be allocated contains one more unit, for the header itself, and this is the value recorded in the `size` field of the header. The pointer returned by `alloc` points at the free space, not at the header itself.

```
      static HEADER base; /* empty list to get started */
      static HEADER *allocp = NULL; /* last allocated block */

      char *alloc(nbytes) /* general-purpose storage allocator */
      unsigned nbytes;
      {
           HEADER *morecore();
           register HEADER *p, *q;
           register int nunits;

           nunits = 1+(nbytes+sizeof(HEADER)-1)/sizeof(HEADER);
           if ((q = allocp) == NULL) {   /* no free list yet */
                base.s.ptr = allocp = q = &base;
                base.s.size = 0;
           }
           for (p=q->s.ptr; ; q=p, p=p->s.ptr) {
                if (p->s.size >= nunits) {   /* big enough */
                     if (p->s.size == nunits) /* exactly */
                          q->s.ptr = p->s.ptr;
                     else {    /* allocate tail end */
                          p->s.size -= nunits;
                          p += p->s.size;
                          p->s.size = nunits;
                     }
                     allocp = q;
                     return((char *)(p+1));
                }
                if (p == allocp)  /* wrapped around free list */
                     if ((p = morecore(nunits)) == NULL)
                          return(NULL);   /* none left */
           }
      }
```

The variable base is used to get started; if allocp is NULL, as it is at
the first call of alloc, then a degenerate free list is created: it contains one
block of size zero, and points to itself. In any case, the free list is then
searched. The search for a free block of adequate size begins at the point
(allocp) where the last block was found; this strategy helps keep the list
homogeneous. If a too-big block is found, the tail end is returned to the
user; in this way the header of the original needs only to have its size
adjusted. In all cases, the pointer returned to the user is to the actual free
area, which is one unit beyond the header. Notice that p is converted to a
character pointer before being returned by alloc.

The function morecore obtains storage from the operating system.
The details of how this is done of course vary from system to system. In
UNIX, the system entry sbrk(n) returns a pointer to n more bytes of
storage. (The pointer satisfies all alignment restrictions.) Since asking the

system for memory is a comparatively expensive operation, we don't want to do that on every call to alloc, so morecore rounds up the number of units requested of it to a larger value; this larger block will be chopped up as needed. The amount of scaling is a parameter that can be tuned as needed.

```
#define    NALLOC    128   /* #units to allocate at once */

static HEADER *morecore(nu)    /* ask system for memory */
unsigned nu;
{
        char *sbrk();
        register char *cp;
        register HEADER *up;
        register int rnu;

        rnu = NALLOC * ((nu+NALLOC-1) / NALLOC);
        cp = sbrk(rnu * sizeof(HEADER));
        if ((int)cp == -1)   /* no space at all */
            return(NULL);
        up = (HEADER *)cp;
        up->s.size = rnu;
        free((char *)(up+1));
        return(allocp);
}
```

sbrk returns −1 if there was no space, even though NULL would have been a better choice. The −1 must be converted to an int so it can be safely compared. Again, casts are heavily used so the function is relatively immune to the details of pointer representation on different machines.

free itself is the last thing. It simply scans the free list, starting at allocp, looking for the place to insert the free block. This is either between two existing blocks or at one end of the list. In any case, if the block being freed is adjacent to either neighbor, the adjacent blocks are combined. The only troubles are keeping the pointers pointing to the right things and the sizes correct.

```
free(ap)   /* put block ap in free list */
char *ap;
{
    register HEADER *p, *q;

    p = (HEADER *)ap - 1;    /* point to header */
    for (q=allocp; !(p > q && p < q->s.ptr); q=q->s.ptr)
        if (q >= q->s.ptr && (p > q || p < q->s.ptr))
            break;    /* at one end or other */

    if (p+p->s.size == q->s.ptr) { /* join to upper nbr */
        p->s.size += q->s.ptr->s.size;
        p->s.ptr = q->s.ptr->s.ptr;
    } else
        p->s.ptr = q->s.ptr;
    if (q+q->s.size == p) {  /* join to lower nbr */
        q->s.size += p->s.size;
        q->s.ptr = p->s.ptr;
    } else
        q->s.ptr = p;
    allocp = q;
}
```

Although storage allocation is intrinsically machine dependent, the code shown above illustrates how the machine dependencies can be controlled and confined to a very small part of the program. The use of typedef and union handles alignment (given that sbrk supplies an appropriate pointer). Casts arrange that pointer conversions are made explicit, and even cope with a badly-designed system interface. Even though the details here are related to storage allocation, the general approach is applicable to other situations as well.

Exercise 8-6. The standard library function calloc(n, size) returns a pointer to n objects of size size, with the storage initialized to zero. Write calloc, using alloc either as a model or as a function to be called. □

Exercise 8-7. alloc accepts a size request without checking its plausibility; free believes that the block it is asked to free contains a valid size field. Improve these routines to take more pains with error checking. □

Exercise 8-8. Write a routine bfree(p, n) which will free an arbitrary block p of n characters into the free list maintained by alloc and free. By using bfree, a user can add a static or external array to the free list at any time. □

APPENDIX A: **C REFERENCE MANUAL**

1. Introduction

This manual describes the C language on the DEC PDP-11, the Honeywell 6000, the IBM System/370, and the Interdata 8/32. Where differences exist, it concentrates on the PDP-11, but tries to point out implementation-dependent details. With few exceptions, these dependencies follow directly from the underlying properties of the hardware; the various compilers are generally quite compatible.

2. Lexical conventions

There are six classes of tokens: identifiers, keywords, constants, strings, operators, and other separators. Blanks, tabs, newlines, and comments (collectively, "white space") as described below are ignored except as they serve to separate tokens. Some white space is required to separate otherwise adjacent identifiers, keywords, and constants.

If the input stream has been parsed into tokens up to a given character, the next token is taken to include the longest string of characters which could possibly constitute a token.

2.1 Comments

The characters /* introduce a comment, which terminates with the characters */. Comments do not nest.

2.2 Identifiers (Names)

An identifier is a sequence of letters and digits; the first character must be a letter. The underscore _ counts as a letter. Upper and lower case letters are different. No more than the first eight characters are significant, although more may be used. External identifiers, which are used by various assemblers and loaders, are more restricted:

DEC PDP-11	7 characters, 2 cases
Honeywell 6000	6 characters, 1 case
IBM 360/370	7 characters, 1 case
Interdata 8/32	8 characters, 2 cases

2.3 Keywords

The following identifiers are reserved for use as keywords, and may not be used otherwise:

```
int        extern     else
char       register   for
float      typedef    do
double     static     while
struct     goto       switch
union      return     case
long       sizeof     default
short      break      entry
unsigned   continue
auto       if
```

The `entry` keyword is not currently implemented by any compiler but is reserved for future use. Some implementations also reserve the words `fortran` and `asm`.

2.4 Constants

There are several kinds of constants, as listed below. Hardware characteristics which affect sizes are summarized in §2.6.

2.4.1 Integer constants

An integer constant consisting of a sequence of digits is taken to be octal if it begins with 0 (digit zero), decimal otherwise. The digits 8 and 9 have octal value 10 and 11 respectively. A sequence of digits preceded by 0x or 0X (digit zero) is taken to be a hexadecimal integer. The hexadecimal digits include a or A through f or F with values 10 through 15. A decimal constant whose value exceeds the largest signed machine integer is taken to be `long`; an octal or hex constant which exceeds the largest unsigned machine integer is likewise taken to be `long`.

2.4.2 Explicit long constants

A decimal, octal, or hexadecimal integer constant immediately followed by l (letter ell) or L is a long constant. As discussed below, on some machines integer and long values may be considered identical.

2.4.3 Character constants

A character constant is a character enclosed in single quotes, as in `'x'`. The value of a character constant is the numerical value of the character in the machine's character set.

Certain non-graphic characters, the single quote `'` and the backslash `\`, may be represented according to the following table of escape sequences:

newline	NL (LF)	\n
horizontal tab	HT	\t
backspace	BS	\b
carriage return	CR	\r
form feed	FF	\f
backslash	\	\\
single quote	'	\'
bit pattern	*ddd*	*ddd*

The escape *ddd* consists of the backslash followed by 1, 2, or 3 octal digits which are taken to specify the value of the desired character. A special case of this construction is \0 (not followed by a digit), which indicates the character NUL. If the character following a backslash is not one of those specified, the backslash is ignored.

2.4.4 Floating constants

A floating constant consists of an integer part, a decimal point, a fraction part, an e or E, and an optionally signed integer exponent. The integer and fraction parts both consist of a sequence of digits. Either the integer part or the fraction part (not both) may be missing; either the decimal point or the e and the exponent (not both) may be missing. Every floating constant is taken to be double-precision.

2.5 Strings

A string is a sequence of characters surrounded by double quotes, as in "...". A string has type "array of characters" and storage class static (see §4 below) and is initialized with the given characters. All strings, even when written identically, are distinct. The compiler places a null byte \0 at the end of each string so that programs which scan the string can find its end. In a string, the double quote character " must be preceded by a \; in addition, the same escapes as described for character constants may be used. Finally, a \ and an immediately following newline are ignored.

2.6 Hardware characteristics

The following table summarizes certain hardware properties which vary from machine to machine. Although these affect program portability, in practice they are less of a problem than might be thought *a priori.*

	DEC PDP-11	Honeywell 6000	IBM 370	Interdata 8/32
	ASCII	ASCII	EBCDIC	ASCII
char	8 bits	9 bits	8 bits	8 bits
int	16	36	32	32
short	16	36	16	16
long	32	36	32	32
float	32	36	32	32
double	64	72	64	64
range	$\pm 10^{\pm 38}$	$\pm 10^{\pm 38}$	$\pm 10^{\pm 76}$	$\pm 10^{\pm 76}$

For these four machines, floating point numbers have 8 bit exponents.

3. Syntax notation

In the syntax notation used in this manual, syntactic categories are indicated by *italic* type, and literal words and characters in **bold** type. Alternative categories are listed on separate lines. An optional terminal or non-terminal symbol is indicated by the subscript "opt," so that

$$\{ \ expression_{opt} \ \}$$

indicates an optional expression enclosed in braces. The syntax is summarized in §18.

4. What's in a name?

C bases the interpretation of an identifier upon two attributes of the identifier: its *storage class* and its *type*. The storage class determines the location and lifetime of the storage associated with an identifier; the type determines the meaning of the values found in the identifier's storage.

There are four declarable storage classes: automatic, static, external, and register. Automatic variables are local to each invocation of a block (§9.2), and are discarded upon exit from the block; static variables are local to a block, but retain their values upon reentry to a block even after control has left the block; external variables exist and retain their values throughout the execution of the entire program, and may be used for communication between functions, even separately compiled functions. Register variables are (if possible) stored in the fast registers of the machine; like automatic variables they are local to each block and disappear on exit from the block.

C supports several fundamental types of objects:

Objects declared as characters (**char**) are large enough to store any member of the implementation's character set, and if a genuine character from that character set is stored in a character variable, its value is equivalent to the integer code for that character. Other quantities may be stored into character variables, but the implementation is machine-dependent.

Up to three sizes of integer, declared **short int**, **int**, and **long int**, are available. Longer integers provide no less storage than shorter ones, but the implementation may make either short integers, or long integers, or both, equivalent to plain integers. "Plain" integers have the natural size suggested by the host machine architecture; the other sizes are provided to meet special needs.

Unsigned integers, declared `unsigned,` obey the laws of arithmetic modulo 2^n where n is the number of bits in the representation. (On the PDP-11, unsigned long quantities are not supported.)

Single-precision floating point (`float`) and double-precision floating point (`double`) may be synonymous in some implementations.

Because objects of the foregoing types can usefully be interpreted as numbers, they will be referred to as *arithmetic* types. Types `char` and `int` of all sizes will collectively be called *integral* types. `float` and `double` will collectively be called *floating* types.

Besides the fundamental arithmetic types there is a conceptually infinite class of derived types constructed from the fundamental types in the following ways:

arrays of objects of most types;

functions which return objects of a given type;

pointers to objects of a given type;

structures containing a sequence of objects of various types;

unions capable of containing any one of several objects of various types.

In general these methods of constructing objects can be applied recursively.

5. Objects and lvalues

An *object* is a manipulatable region of storage; an *lvalue* is an expression referring to an object. An obvious example of an lvalue expression is an identifier. There are operators which yield lvalues: for example, if E is an expression of pointer type, then `*E` is an lvalue expression referring to the object to which E points. The name "lvalue" comes from the assignment expression E1 = E2 in which the left operand E1 must be an lvalue expression. The discussion of each operator below indicates whether it expects lvalue operands and whether it yields an lvalue.

6. Conversions

A number of operators may, depending on their operands, cause conversion of the value of an operand from one type to another. This section explains the result to be expected from such conversions. §6.6 summarizes the conversions demanded by most ordinary operators; it will be supplemented as required by the discussion of each operator.

6.1 Characters and integers

A character or a short integer may be used wherever an integer may be used. In all cases the value is converted to an integer. Conversion of a shorter integer to a longer always involves sign extension; integers are signed quantities. Whether or not sign-extension occurs for characters is machine dependent, but it is guaranteed that a member of the standard character set is non-negative. Of the machines treated by this manual, only the PDP-11 sign-extends. On the PDP-11, character variables range in value from -128 to 127; the characters of the ASCII alphabet are all positive. A character constant specified with an octal escape suffers sign extension and may appear negative; for example, `'\377'` has the value -1.

When a longer integer is converted to a shorter or to a `char,` it is truncated on the left; excess bits are simply discarded.

6.2 Float and double

All floating arithmetic in C is carried out in double-precision; whenever a float appears in an expression it is lengthened to double by zero-padding its fraction. When a double must be converted to float, for example by an assignment, the double is rounded before truncation to float length.

6.3 Floating and integral

Conversions of floating values to integral type tend to be rather machine-dependent; in particular the direction of truncation of negative numbers varies from machine to machine. The result is undefined if the value will not fit in the space provided.

Conversions of integral values to floating type are well behaved. Some loss of precision occurs if the destination lacks sufficient bits.

6.4 Pointers and integers

An integer or long integer may be added to or subtracted from a pointer; in such a case the first is converted as specified in the discussion of the addition operator.

Two pointers to objects of the same type may be subtracted; in this case the result is converted to an integer as specified in the discussion of the subtraction operator.

6.5 Unsigned

Whenever an unsigned integer and a plain integer are combined, the plain integer is converted to unsigned and the result is unsigned. The value is the least unsigned integer congruent to the signed integer (modulo $2^{wordsize}$). In a 2's complement representation, this conversion is conceptual and there is no actual change in the bit pattern.

When an unsigned integer is converted to long, the value of the result is the same numerically as that of the unsigned integer. Thus the conversion amounts to padding with zeros on the left.

6.6 Arithmetic conversions

A great many operators cause conversions and yield result types in a similar way. This pattern will be called the "usual arithmetic conversions."

First, any operands of type char or short are converted to int, and any of type float are converted to double.

Then, if either operand is double, the other is converted to double and that is the type of the result.

Otherwise, if either operand is long, the other is converted to long and that is the type of the result.

Otherwise, if either operand is unsigned, the other is converted to unsigned and that is the type of the result.

Otherwise, both operands must be int, and that is the type of the result.

7. Expressions

The precedence of expression operators is the same as the order of the major subsections of this section, highest precedence first. Thus, for example, the expressions referred to as the operands of + (§7.4) are those expressions defined in §§7.1-7.3. Within each subsection, the operators have the same precedence. Left- or right-associativity is specified in each subsection for the operators discussed therein. The precedence and associativity of all the expression operators is summarized in the grammar of §18.

Otherwise the order of evaluation of expressions is undefined. In particular the compiler considers itself free to compute subexpressions in the order it believes most efficient, even if the subexpressions involve side effects. The order in which side effects take place is unspecified. Expressions involving a commutative and associative operator (*, +, &, |, ^) may be rearranged arbitrarily, even in the presence of parentheses; to force a particular order of evaluation an explicit temporary must be used.

The handling of overflow and divide check in expression evaluation is machine-dependent. All existing implementations of C ignore integer overflows; treatment of division by 0, and all floating-point exceptions, varies between machines, and is usually adjustable by a library function.

7.1 Primary expressions

Primary expressions involving ., ->, subscripting, and function calls group left to right.

> *primary-expression:*
>   *identifier*
>   *constant*
>   *string*
>   (*expression*)
>   *primary-expression* [*expression*]
>   *primary-expression* (*expression-list*$_{opt}$)
>   *primary-lvalue* . *identifier*
>   *primary-expression* -> *identifier*

> *expression-list:*
>   *expression*
>   *expression-list* , *expression*

An identifier is a primary expression, provided it has been suitably declared as discussed below. Its type is specified by its declaration. If the type of the identifier is "array of ...", however, then the value of the identifier-expression is a pointer to the first object in the array, and the type of the expression is "pointer to ...". Moreover, an array identifier is not an lvalue expression. Likewise, an identifier which is declared "function returning ...", when used except in the function-name position of a call, is converted to "pointer to function returning ...".

A constant is a primary expression. Its type may be `int`, `long`, or `double` depending on its form. Character constants have type `int`; floating constants are `double`.

A string is a primary expression. Its type is originally "array of `char`"; but following the same rule given above for identifiers, this is modified to "pointer to `char`" and the result is a pointer to the first character in the string. (There is an exception in certain initializers; see §8.6.)

A parenthesized expression is a primary expression whose type and value are identical to those of the unadorned expression. The presence of parentheses does not affect whether the expression is an lvalue.

A primary expression followed by an expression in square brackets is a primary expression. The intuitive meaning is that of a subscript. Usually, the primary expression has type "pointer to ...", the subscript expression is `int`, and the type of the result is "...". The expression `E1[E2]` is identical (by definition) to `*((E1)+(E2))`. All the clues needed to understand this notation are contained in this section together with the discussions in §§ 7.1, 7.2, and 7.4 on identifiers, `*`, and + respectively; §14.3 below summarizes the implications.

A function call is a primary expression followed by parentheses containing a possibly empty, comma-separated list of expressions which constitute the actual arguments to the function. The primary expression must be of type "function returning ...", and the result of the function call is of type "...". As indicated below, a hitherto unseen identifier followed immediately by a left parenthesis is contextually declared to represent a function returning an integer; thus in the most common case, integer-valued functions need not be declared.

Any actual arguments of type `float` are converted to `double` before the call; any of type `char` or `short` are converted to `int`; and as usual, array names are converted to pointers. No other conversions are performed automatically; in particular, the compiler does not compare the types of actual arguments with those of formal arguments. If conversion is needed, use a cast; see §7.2, 8.7.

In preparing for the call to a function, a copy is made of each actual parameter; thus, all argument-passing in C is strictly by value. A function may change the values of its formal parameters, but these changes cannot affect the values of the actual parameters. On the other hand, it is possible to pass a pointer on the understanding that the function may change the value of the object to which the pointer points. An array name is a pointer expression. The order of evaluation of arguments is undefined by the language; take note that the various compilers differ.

Recursive calls to any function are permitted.

A primary expression followed by a dot followed by an identifier is an expression. The first expression must be an lvalue naming a structure or a union, and the identifier must name a member of the structure or union. The result is an lvalue referring to the named member of the structure or union.

A primary expression followed by an arrow (built from a – and a >) followed by an identifier is an expression. The first expression must be a pointer to a structure or a union and the identifier must name a member of that structure or union. The result is an lvalue referring to the named member of the structure or union to which the pointer expression points.

Thus the expression `E1->MOS` is the same as `(*E1).MOS`. Structures and unions are discussed in §8.5. The rules given here for the use of structures and unions are not enforced strictly, in order to allow an escape from the typing mechanism. See §14.1.

7.2 Unary operators

Expressions with unary operators group right-to-left.

> *unary-expression:*
>> * *expression*
>> & *lvalue*
>> − *expression*
>> ! *expression*
>> ~ *expression*
>> ++ *lvalue*
>> −− *lvalue*
>> *lvalue* ++
>> *lvalue* −−
>> (*type-name*) *expression*
>> `sizeof` *expression*
>> `sizeof` (*type-name*)

The unary * operator means *indirection*: the expression must be a pointer, and the result is an lvalue referring to the object to which the expression points. If the type of the expression is "pointer to ...", the type of the result is "...".

The result of the unary & operator is a pointer to the object referred to by the lvalue. If the type of the lvalue is "...", the type of the result is "pointer to ...".

The result of the unary − operator is the negative of its operand. The usual arithmetic conversions are performed. The negative of an unsigned quantity is computed by subtracting its value from 2^n, where *n* is the number of bits in an `int`. There is no unary + operator.

The result of the logical negation operator ! is 1 if the value of its operand is 0, 0 if the value of its operand is non-zero. The type of the result is `int`. It is applicable to any arithmetic type or to pointers.

The ~ operator yields the one's complement of its operand. The usual arithmetic conversions are performed. The type of the operand must be integral.

The object referred to by the lvalue operand of prefix ++ is incremented. The value is the new value of the operand, but is not an lvalue. The expression ++x is equivalent to x+=1. See the discussions of addition (§7.4) and assignment operators (§7.14) for information on conversions.

The lvalue operand of prefix −− is decremented analogously to the prefix ++ operator.

When postfix ++ is applied to an lvalue the result is the value of the object referred to by the lvalue. After the result is noted, the object is incremented in the same manner as for the prefix ++ operator. The type of the result is the same as the type of the lvalue expression.

When postfix −− is applied to an lvalue the result is the value of the object referred to by the lvalue. After the result is noted, the object is decremented in the manner as for the prefix −− operator. The type of the result is the same as the type of the lvalue expression.

An expression preceded by the parenthesized name of a data type causes conversion of the value of the expression to the named type. This construction is called a *cast*. Type names are described in §8.7.

The `sizeof` operator yields the size, in bytes, of its operand. (A *byte* is undefined by the language except in terms of the value of `sizeof`. However, in all existing implementations a byte is the space required to hold a `char`.) When applied to an array, the result is the total number of bytes in the array. The size is determined from the declarations of the objects in the expression. This expression is semantically an integer constant and may be used anywhere a constant is required. Its major use is in communication with routines like storage allocators and I/O systems.

The `sizeof` operator may also be applied to a parenthesized type name. In that case it yields the size, in bytes, of an object of the indicated type.

The construction `sizeof(`*type*`)` is taken to be a unit, so the expression `sizeof(`*type*`)-2` is the same as `(sizeof(`*type*`))-2`.

7.3 Multiplicative operators

The multiplicative operators `*`, `/`, and `%` group left-to-right. The usual arithmetic conversions are performed.

> *multiplicative-expression:*
>   *expression* `*` *expression*
>   *expression* `/` *expression*
>   *expression* `%` *expression*

The binary `*` operator indicates multiplication. The `*` operator is associative and expressions with several multiplications at the same level may be rearranged by the compiler.

The binary `/` operator indicates division. When positive integers are divided truncation is toward 0, but the form of truncation is machine-dependent if either operand is negative. On all machines covered by this manual, the remainder has the same sign as the dividend. It is always true that `(a/b)*b + a%b` is equal to `a` (if `b` is not 0).

The binary `%` operator yields the remainder from the division of the first expression by the second. The usual arithmetic conversions are performed. The operands must not be `float`.

7.4 Additive operators

The additive operators `+` and `-` group left-to-right. The usual arithmetic conversions are performed. There are some additional type possibilities for each operator.

> *additive-expression:*
>   *expression* `+` *expression*
>   *expression* `-` *expression*

The result of the `+` operator is the sum of the operands. A pointer to an object in an array and a value of any integral type may be added. The latter is in all cases converted to an address offset by multiplying it by the length of the object to which the pointer points. The result is a pointer of the same type as the original pointer, and which points to another object in the same array, appropriately offset from the original object. Thus if `P` is a pointer to an object in an array, the expression `P+1` is a pointer to the next object in the array.

No further type combinations are allowed for pointers.

The + operator is associative and expressions with several additions at the same level may be rearranged by the compiler.

The result of the − operator is the difference of the operands. The usual arithmetic conversions are performed. Additionally, a value of any integral type may be subtracted from a pointer, and then the same conversions as for addition apply.

If two pointers to objects of the same type are subtracted, the result is converted (by division by the length of the object) to an int representing the number of objects separating the pointed-to objects. This conversion will in general give unexpected results unless the pointers point to objects in the same array, since pointers, even to objects of the same type, do not necessarily differ by a multiple of the object-length.

7.5 Shift operators

The shift operators << and >> group left-to-right. Both perform the usual arithmetic conversions on their operands, each of which must be integral. Then the right operand is converted to int; the type of the result is that of the left operand. The result is undefined if the right operand is negative, or greater than or equal to the length of the object in bits.

> *shift-expression:*
> *expression* << *expression*
> *expression* >> *expression*

The value of E1<<E2 is E1 (interpreted as a bit pattern) left-shifted E2 bits; vacated bits are 0-filled. The value of E1>>E2 is E1 right-shifted E2 bit positions. The right shift is guaranteed to be logical (0-fill) if E1 is unsigned; otherwise it may be (and is, on the PDP-11) arithmetic (fill by a copy of the sign bit).

7.6 Relational operators

The relational operators group left-to-right, but this fact is not very useful; a<b<c does not mean what it seems to.

> *relational-expression:*
> *expression* < *expression*
> *expression* > *expression*
> *expression* <= *expression*
> *expression* >= *expression*

The operators < (less than), > (greater than), <= (less than or equal to) and >= (greater than or equal to) all yield 0 if the specified relation is false and 1 if it is true. The type of the result is int. The usual arithmetic conversions are performed. Two pointers may be compared; the result depends on the relative locations in the address space of the pointed-to objects. Pointer comparison is portable only when the pointers point to objects in the same array.

7.7 Equality operators

> *equality-expression:*
>> *expression* == *expression*
>> *expression* ! = *expression*

The == (equal to) and the ! = (not equal to) operators are exactly analogous to the relational operators except for their lower precedence. (Thus a<b == c<d is 1 whenever a<b and c<d have the same truth-value).

A pointer may be compared to an integer, but the result is machine dependent unless the integer is the constant 0. A pointer to which 0 has been assigned is guaranteed not to point to any object, and will appear to be equal to 0; in conventional usage, such a pointer is considered to be null.

7.8 Bitwise AND operator

> *and-expression:*
>> *expression* & *expression*

The & operator is associative and expressions involving & may be rearranged. The usual arithmetic conversions are performed; the result is the bitwise AND function of the operands. The operator applies only to integral operands.

7.9 Bitwise exclusive OR operator

> *exclusive-or-expression:*
>> *expression* ^ *expression*

The ^ operator is associative and expressions involving ^ may be rearranged. The usual arithmetic conversions are performed; the result is the bitwise exclusive OR function of the operands. The operator applies only to integral operands.

7.10 Bitwise inclusive OR operator

> *inclusive-or-expression:*
>> *expression* | *expression*

The | operator is associative and expressions involving | may be rearranged. The usual arithmetic conversions are performed; the result is the bitwise inclusive OR function of its operands. The operator applies only to integral operands.

7.11 Logical AND operator

> *logical-and-expression:*
>> *expression* && *expression*

The && operator groups left-to-right. It returns 1 if both its operands are non-zero, 0 otherwise. Unlike &, && guarantees left-to-right evaluation; moreover the second operand is not evaluated if the first operand is 0.

The operands need not have the same type, but each must have one of the fundamental types or be a pointer. The result is always int.

7.12 Logical OR operator

> *logical-or-expression:*
>   *expression* | | *expression*

The | | operator groups left-to-right. It returns 1 if either of its operands is non-zero, and 0 otherwise. Unlike |, | | guarantees left-to-right evaluation; moreover, the second operand is not evaluated if the value of the first operand is non-zero.

The operands need not have the same type, but each must have one of the fundamental types or be a pointer. The result is always int.

7.13 Conditional operator

> *conditional-expression:*
>   *expression* ? *expression* : *expression*

Conditional expressions group right-to-left. The first expression is evaluated and if it is non-zero, the result is the value of the second expression, otherwise that of third expression. If possible, the usual arithmetic conversions are performed to bring the second and third expressions to a common type; otherwise, if both are pointers of the same type, the result has the common type; otherwise, one must be a pointer and the other the constant 0, and the result has the type of the pointer. Only one of the second and third expressions is evaluated.

7.14 Assignment operators

There are a number of assignment operators, all of which group right-to-left. All require an lvalue as their left operand, and the type of an assignment expression is that of its left operand. The value is the value stored in the left operand after the assignment has taken place. The two parts of a compound assignment operator are separate tokens.

> *assignment-expression:*
>   *lvalue* = *expression*
>   *lvalue* += *expression*
>   *lvalue* −= *expression*
>   *lvalue* *= *expression*
>   *lvalue* /= *expression*
>   *lvalue* %= *expression*
>   *lvalue* >>= *expression*
>   *lvalue* <<= *expression*
>   *lvalue* &= *expression*
>   *lvalue* ^= *expression*
>   *lvalue* |= *expression*

In the simple assignment with =, the value of the expression replaces that of the object referred to by the lvalue. If both operands have arithmetic type, the right operand is converted to the type of the left preparatory to the assignment.

The behavior of an expression of the form E1 *op*= E2 may be inferred by taking it as equivalent to E1 = E1 *op* (E2); however, E1 is evaluated only once. In += and −=, the left operand may be a pointer, in which case the (integral) right operand is converted as explained in §7.4; all right operands and all non-pointer left operands must have arithmetic type.

The compilers currently allow a pointer to be assigned to an integer, an integer to a pointer, and a pointer to a pointer of another type. The assignment is a pure copy operation, with no conversion. This usage is nonportable, and may produce pointers which cause addressing exceptions when used. However, it is guaranteed that assignment of the constant 0 to a pointer will produce a null pointer distinguishable from a pointer to any object.

7.15 Comma operator

> *comma-expression:*
> *expression , expression*

A pair of expressions separated by a comma is evaluated left-to-right and the value of the left expression is discarded. The type and value of the result are the type and value of the right operand. This operator groups left-to-right. In contexts where comma is given a special meaning, for example in a list of actual arguments to functions (§7.1) and lists of initializers (§8.6), the comma operator as described in this section can only appear in parentheses; for example,

```
f(a, (t=3, t+2), c)
```

has three arguments, the second of which has the value 5.

8. Declarations

Declarations are used to specify the interpretation which C gives to each identifier; they do not necessarily reserve storage associated with the identifier. Declarations have the form

> *declaration:*
> *decl-specifiers declarator-list$_{opt}$;*

The declarators in the declarator-list contain the identifiers being declared. The decl-specifiers consist of a sequence of type and storage class specifiers.

> *decl-specifiers:*
> *type-specifier decl-specifiers$_{opt}$*
> *sc-specifier decl-specifiers$_{opt}$*

The list must be self-consistent in a way described below.

8.1 Storage class specifiers

The sc-specifiers are:

> *sc-specifier:*
> ```
> auto
> static
> extern
> register
> typedef
> ```

The `typedef` specifier does not reserve storage and is called a "storage class specifier" only for syntactic convenience; it is discussed in §8.8. The meanings of the various storage classes were discussed in §4.

The `auto`, `static`, and `register` declarations also serve as definitions in that they cause an appropriate amount of storage to be reserved. In the `extern` case there must be an external definition (§10) for the given identifiers somewhere outside the function in which they are declared.

A `register` declaration is best thought of as an `auto` declaration, together with a hint to the compiler that the variables declared will be heavily used. Only the first few such declarations are effective. Moreover, only variables of certain types will be stored in registers; on the PDP-11, they are `int`, `char`, or pointer. One other restriction applies to register variables: the address-of operator `&` cannot be applied to them. Smaller, faster programs can be expected if register declarations are used appropriately, but future improvements in code generation may render them unnecessary.

At most one sc-specifier may be given in a declaration. If the sc-specifier is missing from a declaration, it is taken to be `auto` inside a function, `extern` outside. Exception: functions are never automatic.

8.2 Type specifiers

The type-specifiers are

> *type-specifier:*
>   `char`
>   `short`
>   `int`
>   `long`
>   `unsigned`
>   `float`
>   `double`
>   *struct-or-union-specifier*
>   *typedef-name*

The words `long`, `short`, and `unsigned` may be thought of as adjectives; the following combinations are acceptable.

> `short int`
> `long int`
> `unsigned int`
> `long float`

The meaning of the last is the same as `double`. Otherwise, at most one type-specifier may be given in a declaration. If the type-specifier is missing from a declaration, it is taken to be `int`.

Specifiers for structures and unions are discussed in §8.5; declarations with `typedef` names are discussed in §8.8.

8.3 Declarators

The declarator-list appearing in a declaration is a comma-separated sequence of declarators, each of which may have an initializer.

> *declarator-list:*
> > *init-declarator*
> > *init-declarator , declarator-list*

> *init-declarator:*
> > *declarator initializer*$_{opt}$

Initializers are discussed in §8.6. The specifiers in the declaration indicate the type and storage class of the objects to which the declarators refer. Declarators have the syntax:

> *declarator:*
> > *identifier*
> > *(declarator)*
> > ∗ *declarator*
> > *declarator ( )*
> > *declarator [constant-expression*$_{opt}$ *]*

The grouping is the same as in expressions.

8.4 Meaning of declarators

Each declarator is taken to be an assertion that when a construction of the same form as the declarator appears in an expression, it yields an object of the indicated type and storage class. Each declarator contains exactly one identifier; it is this identifier that is declared.

If an unadorned identifier appears as a declarator, then it has the type indicated by the specifier heading the declaration.

A declarator in parentheses is identical to the unadorned declarator, but the binding of complex declarators may be altered by parentheses. See the examples below.

Now imagine a declaration

        T D1

where T is a type-specifier (like `int`, etc.) and D1 is a declarator. Suppose this declaration makes the identifier have type "... T," where the "..." is empty if D1 is just a plain identifier (so that the type of x in "`int x`" is just `int`). Then if D1 has the form

        ∗D

the type of the contained identifier is "... pointer to T."

If D1 has the form

        D()

then the contained identifier has the type "... function returning T."

If D1 has the form

        D[*constant-expression*]

or

```
D[]
```

then the contained identifier has type "... array of T." In the first case the constant expression is an expression whose value is determinable at compile time, and whose type is int. (Constant expressions are defined precisely in §15.) When several "array of" specifications are adjacent, a multi-dimensional array is created; the constant expressions which specify the bounds of the arrays may be missing only for the first member of the sequence. This elision is useful when the array is external and the actual definition, which allocates storage, is given elsewhere. The first constant-expression may also be omitted when the declarator is followed by initialization. In this case the size is calculated from the number of initial elements supplied.

An array may be constructed from one of the basic types, from a pointer, from a structure or union, or from another array (to generate a multi-dimensional array).

Not all the possibilities allowed by the syntax above are actually permitted. The restrictions are as follows: functions may not return arrays, structures, unions or functions, although they may return pointers to such things; there are no arrays of functions, although there may be arrays of pointers to functions. Likewise a structure or union may not contain a function, but it may contain a pointer to a function.

As an example, the declaration

```
int i, *ip, f(), *fip(), (*pfi)();
```

declares an integer i, a pointer ip to an integer, a function f returning an integer, a function fip returning a pointer to an integer, and a pointer pfi to a function which returns an integer. It is especially useful to compare the last two. The binding of *fip() is *(fip()), so that the declaration suggests, and the same construction in an expression requires, the calling of a function fip, and then using indirection through the (pointer) result to yield an integer. In the declarator (*pfi)(), the extra parentheses are necessary, as they are also in an expression, to indicate that indirection through a pointer to a function yields a function, which is then called; it returns an integer.

As another example,

```
float fa[17], *afp[17];
```

declares an array of float numbers and an array of pointers to float numbers. Finally,

```
static int x3d[3][5][7];
```

declares a static three-dimensional array of integers, with rank 3×5×7. In complete detail, x3d is an array of three items; each item is an array of five arrays; each of the latter arrays is an array of seven integers. Any of the expressions x3d, x3d[i], x3d[i][j], x3d[i][j][k] may reasonably appear in an expression. The first three have type "array," the last has type int.

8.5 Structure and union declarations

A structure is an object consisting of a sequence of named members. Each member may have any type. A union is an object which may, at a given time, contain any one of several members. Structure and union specifiers have the same form.

> *struct-or-union-specifier:*
>> *struct-or-union { struct-decl-list }*
>> *struct-or-union identifier { struct-decl-list }*
>> *struct-or-union identifier*

> *struct-or-union:*
>> `struct`
>> `union`

The struct-decl-list is a sequence of declarations for the members of the structure or union:

> *struct-decl-list:*
>> *struct-declaration*
>> *struct-declaration struct-decl-list*

> *struct-declaration:*
>> *type-specifier struct-declarator-list ;*

> *struct-declarator-list:*
>> *struct-declarator*
>> *struct-declarator , struct-declarator-list*

In the usual case, a struct-declarator is just a declarator for a member of a structure or union. A structure member may also consist of a specified number of bits. Such a member is also called a *field*; its length is set off from the field name by a colon.

> *struct-declarator:*
>> *declarator*
>> *declarator : constant-expression*
>> *: constant-expression*

Within a structure, the objects declared have addresses which increase as their declarations are read left-to-right. Each non-field member of a structure begins on an addressing boundary appropriate to its type; therefore, there may be unnamed holes in a structure. Field members are packed into machine integers; they do not straddle words. A field which does not fit into the space remaining in a word is put into the next word. No field may be wider than a word. Fields are assigned right-to-left on the PDP-11, left-to-right on other machines.

A struct-declarator with no declarator, only a colon and a width, indicates an unnamed field useful for padding to conform to externally-imposed layouts. As a special case, an unnamed field with a width of 0 specifies alignment of the next field at a word boundary. The "next field" presumably is a field, not an ordinary structure member, because in the latter case the alignment would have been automatic.

The language does not restrict the types of things that are declared as fields, but implementations are not required to support any but integer fields. Moreover, even `int` fields may be considered to be unsigned. On the PDP-11, fields are not signed and have only integer values. In all implementations, there are no arrays of fields, and the address-of operator `&` may not be applied to them, so that there are no pointers to fields.

A union may be thought of as a structure all of whose members begin at offset 0 and whose size is sufficient to contain any of its members. At most one of the members can be stored in a union at any time.

A structure or union specifier of the second form, that is, one of

> struct *identifier* { *struct-decl-list* }
> union *identifier* { *struct-decl-list* }

declares the identifier to be the *structure tag* (or union tag) of the structure specified by the list. A subsequent declaration may then use the third form of specifier, one of

> struct *identifier*
> union *identifier*

Structure tags allow definition of self-referential structures; they also permit the long part of the declaration to be given once and used several times. It is illegal to declare a structure or union which contains an instance of itself, but a structure or union may contain a pointer to an instance of itself.

The names of members and tags may be the same as ordinary variables. However, names of tags and members must be mutually distinct.

Two structures may share a common initial sequence of members; that is, the same member may appear in two different structures if it has the same type in both and if all previous members are the same in both. (Actually, the compiler checks only that a name in two different structures has the same type and offset in both, but if preceding members differ the construction is nonportable.)

A simple example of a structure declaration is

```
struct tnode {
    char tword[20];
    int count;
    struct tnode *left;
    struct tnode *right;
};
```

which contains an array of 20 characters, an integer, and two pointers to similar structures. Once this declaration has been given, the declaration

```
struct tnode s, *sp;
```

declares s to be a structure of the given sort and sp to be a pointer to a structure of the given sort. With these declarations, the expression

```
sp->count
```

refers to the count field of the structure to which sp points;

```
        s.left
```

refers to the left subtree pointer of the structure s; and

```
        s.right->tword[0]
```

refers to the first character of the tword member of the right subtree of s.

8.6 Initialization

A declarator may specify an initial value for the identifier being declared. The initializer is preceded by =, and consists of an expression or a list of values nested in braces.

> *initializer:*
>   = *expression*
>   = { *initializer-list* }
>   = { *initializer-list* , }

> *initializer-list:*
>   *expression*
>   *initializer-list* , *initializer-list*
>   { *initializer-list* }

All the expressions in an initializer for a static or external variable must be constant expressions, which are described in §15, or expressions which reduce to the address of a previously declared variable, possibly offset by a constant expression. Automatic or register variables may be initialized by arbitrary expressions involving constants, and previously declared variables and functions.

Static and external variables which are not initialized are guaranteed to start off as 0; automatic and register variables which are not initialized are guaranteed to start off as garbage.

When an initializer applies to a *scalar* (a pointer or an object of arithmetic type), it consists of a single expression, perhaps in braces. The initial value of the object is taken from the expression; the same conversions as for assignment are performed.

When the declared variable is an *aggregate* (a structure or array) then the initializer consists of a brace-enclosed, comma-separated list of initializers for the members of the aggregate, written in increasing subscript or member order. If the aggregate contains subaggregates, this rule applies recursively to the members of the aggregate. If there are fewer initializers in the list than there are members of the aggregate, then the aggregate is padded with 0's. It is not permitted to initialize unions or automatic aggregates.

Braces may be elided as follows. If the initializer begins with a left brace, then the succeeding comma-separated list of initializers initializes the members of the aggregate; it is erroneous for there to be more initializers than members. If, however, the initializer does not begin with a left brace, then only enough elements from the list are taken to account for the members of the aggregate; any remaining members are left to initialize the next member of the aggregate of which the current aggregate is a part.

A final abbreviation allows a `char` array to be initialized by a string. In this case successive characters of the string initialize the members of the array.

For example,

```
int x[] = { 1, 3, 5 };
```

declares and initializes `x` as a 1-dimensional array which has three members, since no size was specified and there are three initializers.

```
float y[4][3] = {
     { 1, 3, 5 },
     { 2, 4, 6 },
     { 3, 5, 7 },
};
```

is a completely-bracketed initialization: 1, 3, and 5 initialize the first row of the array `y[0]`, namely `y[0][0]`, `y[0][1]`, and `y[0][2]`. Likewise the next two lines initialize `y[1]` and `y[2]`. The initializer ends early and therefore `y[3]` is initialized with 0. Precisely the same effect could have been achieved by

```
float y[4][3] = {
     1, 3, 5, 2, 4, 6, 3, 5, 7
};
```

The initializer for `y` begins with a left brace, but that for `y[0]` does not, therefore 3 elements from the list are used. Likewise the next three are taken successively for `y[1]` and `y[2]`. Also,

```
float y[4][3] = {
     { 1 }, { 2 }, { 3 }, { 4 }
};
```

initializes the first column of `y` (regarded as a two-dimensional array) and leaves the rest 0.

Finally,

```
char msg[] = "Syntax error on line %s\n";
```

shows a character array whose members are initialized with a string.

8.7 Type names

In two contexts (to specify type conversions explicitly by means of a cast, and as an argument of `sizeof`) it is desired to supply the name of a data type. This is accomplished using a "type name," which in essence is a declaration for an object of that type which omits the name of the object.

> *type-name:*
> *type-specifier abstract-declarator*

> *abstract-declarator:*
>> *empty*
>> (*abstract-declarator*)
>> * *abstract-declarator*
>> *abstract-declarator* ( )
>> *abstract-declarator* [*constant-expression*$_{opt}$]

To avoid ambiguity, in the construction

> (*abstract-declarator*)

the abstract-declarator is required to be non-empty. Under this restriction, it is possible to identify uniquely the location in the abstract-declarator where the identifier would appear if the construction were a declarator in a declaration. The named type is then the same as the type of the hypothetical identifier. For example,

```
int
int *
int *[3]
int (*) [3]
int *()
int (*) ()
```

name respectively the types "integer," "pointer to integer," "array of 3 pointers to integers," "pointer to an array of 3 integers," "function returning pointer to integer," and "pointer to function returning an integer."

8.8 Typedef

Declarations whose "storage class" is `typedef` do not define storage, but instead define identifiers which can be used later as if they were type keywords naming fundamental or derived types.

> *typedef-name:*
>> *identifier*

Within the scope of a declaration involving `typedef`, each identifier appearing as part of any declarator therein become syntactically equivalent to the type keyword naming the type associated with the identifier in the way described in §8.4. For example, after

```
typedef int MILES, *KLICKSP;
typedef struct { double re, im;} complex;
```

the constructions

```
MILES distance;
extern KLICKSP metricp;
complex z, *zp;
```

are all legal declarations; the type of `distance` is `int`, that of `metricp` is "pointer to `int`," and that of `z` is the specified structure. `zp` is a pointer to such a structure.

`typedef` does not introduce brand new types, only synonyms for types which could be specified in another way. Thus in the example above `distance` is considered to have exactly the same type as any other `int` object.

9. Statements

Except as indicated, statements are executed in sequence.

9.1 Expression statement

Most statements are expression statements, which have the form

expression ;

Usually expression statements are assignments or function calls.

9.2 Compound statement, or block

So that several statements can be used where one is expected, the compound statement (also, and equivalently, called "block") is provided:

compound-statement:
{ *declaration-list*$_{opt}$ *statement-list*$_{opt}$ }

declaration-list:
declaration
declaration declaration-list

statement-list:
statement
statement statement-list

If any of the identifiers in the declaration-list were previously declared, the outer declaration is pushed down for the duration of the block, after which it resumes its force.

Any initializations of `auto` or `register` variables are performed each time the block is entered at the top. It is currently possible (but a bad practice) to transfer into a block; in that case the initializations are not performed. Initializations of `static` variables are performed only once when the program begins execution. Inside a block, `extern` declarations do not reserve storage so initialization is not permitted.

9.3 Conditional statement

The two forms of the conditional statement are

`if` (*expression*) *statement*
`if` (*expression*) *statement* `else` *statement*

In both cases the expression is evaluated and if it is non-zero, the first substatement is executed. In the second case the second substatement is executed if the expression is 0. As usual the "else" ambiguity is resolved by connecting an `else` with the last encountered `else`-less `if`.

9.4 While statement
The `while` statement has the form

> `while` (*expression*) *statement*

The substatement is executed repeatedly so long as the value of the expression remains non-zero. The test takes place before each execution of the statement.

9.5 Do statement
The `do` statement has the form

> `do` *statement* `while` (*expression*) `;`

The substatement is executed repeatedly until the value of the expression becomes zero. The test takes place after each execution of the statement.

9.6 For statement
The `for` statement has the form

> `for` (*expression-1*$_{opt}$; *expression-2*$_{opt}$; *expression-3*$_{opt}$) *statement*

This statement is equivalent to

> *expression-1* ;
> `while` (*expression-2*) {
>   *statement*
>   *expression-3* ;
> }

Thus the first expression specifies initialization for the loop; the second specifies a test, made before each iteration, such that the loop is exited when the expression becomes 0; the third expression often specifies an incrementation which is performed after each iteration.

Any or all of the expressions may be dropped. A missing *expression-2* makes the implied `while` clause equivalent to `while(1)`; other missing expressions are simply dropped from the expansion above.

9.7 Switch statement
The `switch` statement causes control to be transferred to one of several statements depending on the value of an expression. It has the form

> `switch` (*expression*) *statement*

The usual arithmetic conversion is performed on the expression, but the result must be `int`. The statement is typically compound. Any statement within the statement may be labeled with one or more case prefixes as follows:

> `case` *constant-expression* :

where the constant expression must be `int`. No two of the case constants in the same switch may have the same value. Constant expressions are precisely defined in §15.

There may also be at most one statement prefix of the form

```
        default :
```

When the `switch` statement is executed, its expression is evaluated and compared with each case constant. If one of the case constants is equal to the value of the expression, control is passed to the statement following the matched case prefix. If no case constant matches the expression, and if there is a `default` prefix, control passes to the prefixed statement. If no case matches and if there is no `default` then none of the statements in the switch is executed.

    `case` and `default` prefixes in themselves do not alter the flow of control, which continues unimpeded across such prefixes. To exit from a switch, see `break`, §9.8.

    Usually the statement that is the subject of a switch is compound. Declarations may appear at the head of this statement, but initializations of automatic or register variables are ineffective.

9.8 Break statement
    The statement

```
        break ;
```

causes termination of the smallest enclosing `while`, `do`, `for`, or `switch` statement; control passes to the statement following the terminated statement.

9.9 Continue statement
    The statement

```
        continue ;
```

causes control to pass to the loop-continuation portion of the smallest enclosing `while`, `do`, or `for` statement; that is to the end of the loop. More precisely, in each of the statements

```
while (...) {        do {                for (...) {
    ...                 ...                 ...
contin: ;           contin: ;           contin: ;
}                   } while (...);       }
```

a `continue` is equivalent to `goto contin`. (Following the `contin:` is a null statement, §9.13.)

9.10 Return statement
    A function returns to its caller by means of the `return` statement, which has one of the forms

```
        return ;
        return expression ;
```

In the first case the returned value is undefined. In the second case, the value of the expression is returned to the caller of the function. If required, the expression is converted, as if by assignment, to the type of the function in which it appears. Flowing off the end of a function is equivalent to a return with no returned value.

9.11 Goto statement

Control may be transferred unconditionally by means of the statement

goto *identifier* ;

The identifier must be a label (§9.12) located in the current function.

9.12 Labeled statement

Any statement may be preceded by label prefixes of the form

identifier :

which serve to declare the identifier as a label. The only use of a label is as a target of a goto. The scope of a label is the current function, excluding any sub-blocks in which the same identifier has been redeclared. See §11.

9.13 Null statement

The null statement has the form

;

A null statement is useful to carry a label just before the } of a compound statement or to supply a null body to a looping statement such as while.

10. External definitions

A C program consists of a sequence of external definitions. An external definition declares an identifier to have storage class extern (by default) or perhaps static, and a specified type. The type-specifier (§8.2) may also be empty, in which case the type is taken to be int. The scope of external definitions persists to the end of the file in which they are declared just as the effect of declarations persists to the end of a block. The syntax of external definitions is the same as that of all declarations, except that only at this level may the code for functions be given.

10.1 External function definitions

Function definitions have the form

> *function-definition:*
>> *decl-specifiers$_{opt}$ function-declarator function-body*

The only sc-specifiers allowed among the decl-specifiers are extern or static; see §11.2 for the distinction between them. A function declarator is similar to a declarator for a "function returning ..." except that it lists the formal parameters of the function being defined.

> *function-declarator:*
>> *declarator (parameter-list$_{opt}$)*

> *parameter-list:*
>> *identifier*
>> *identifier , parameter-list*

The function-body has the form

function-body:
    declaration-list compound-statement

The identifiers in the parameter list, and only those identifiers, may be declared in the declaration list. Any identifiers whose type is not given are taken to be `int`. The only storage class which may be specified is `register`; if it is specified, the corresponding actual parameter will be copied, if possible, into a register at the outset of the function.

A simple example of a complete function definition is

```
int max(a, b, c)
int a, b, c;
{
        int m;

        m = (a > b) ? a : b;
        return((m > c) ? m : c);
}
```

Here `int` is the type-specifier; `max(a, b, c)` is the function-declarator; `int a, b, c;` is the declaration-list for the formal parameters; { ... } is the block giving the code for the statement.

C converts all `float` actual parameters to `double`, so formal parameters declared `float` have their declaration adjusted to read `double`. Also, since a reference to an array in any context (in particular as an actual parameter) is taken to mean a pointer to the first element of the array, declarations of formal parameters declared "array of ..." are adjusted to read "pointer to ...". Finally, because structures, unions and functions cannot be passed to a function, it is useless to declare a formal parameter to be a structure, union or function (pointers to such objects are of course permitted).

10.2 External data definitions

An external data definition has the form

data-definition:
    declaration

The storage class of such data may be `extern` (which is the default) or `static`, but not `auto` or `register`.

11. Scope rules

A C program need not all be compiled at the same time: the source text of the program may be kept in several files, and precompiled routines may be loaded from libraries. Communication among the functions of a program may be carried out both through explicit calls and through manipulation of external data.

Therefore, there are two kinds of scope to consider: first, what may be called the *lexical scope* of an identifier, which is essentially the region of a program during which it may be used without drawing "undefined identifier" diagnostics; and second, the scope associated with external identifiers, which is characterized by the rule that references to the same external identifier are references to the same object.

11.1 Lexical scope

The lexical scope of identifiers declared in external definitions persists from the definition through the end of the source file in which they appear. The lexical scope of identifiers which are formal parameters persists through the function with which they are associated. The lexical scope of identifiers declared at the head of blocks persists until the end of the block. The lexical scope of labels is the whole of the function in which they appear.

Because all references to the same external identifier refer to the same object (see §11.2) the compiler checks all declarations of the same external identifier for compatibility; in effect their scope is increased to the whole file in which they appear.

In all cases, however, if an identifier is explicitly declared at the head of a block, including the block constituting a function, any declaration of that identifier outside the block is suspended until the end of the block.

Remember also (§8.5) that identifiers associated with ordinary variables on the one hand and those associated with structure and union members and tags on the other form two disjoint classes which do not conflict. Members and tags follow the same scope rules as other identifiers. `typedef` names are in the same class as ordinary identifiers. They may be redeclared in inner blocks, but an explicit type must be given in the inner declaration:

```
typedef float distance;
...
{
        auto int distance;
        ...
```

The `int` must be present in the second declaration, or it would be taken to be a declaration with no declarators and type `distance`†.

11.2 Scope of externals

If a function refers to an identifier declared to be `extern`, then somewhere among the files or libraries constituting the complete program there must be an external definition for the identifier. All functions in a given program which refer to the same external identifier refer to the same object, so care must be taken that the type and size specified in the definition are compatible with those specified by each function which references the data.

The appearance of the `extern` keyword in an external definition indicates that storage for the identifiers being declared will be allocated in another file. Thus in a multi-file program, an external data definition without the `extern` specifier must appear in exactly one of the files. Any other files which wish to give an external definition for the identifier must include the `extern` in the definition. The identifier can be initialized only in the declaration where storage is allocated.

Identifiers declared `static` at the top level in external definitions are not visible in other files. Functions may be declared `static`.

---

†It is agreed that the ice is thin here.

12. Compiler control lines

The C compiler contains a preprocessor capable of macro substitution, conditional compilation, and inclusion of named files. Lines beginning with # communicate with this preprocessor. These lines have syntax independent of the rest of the language; they may appear anywhere and have effect which lasts (independent of scope) until the end of the source program file.

12.1 Token replacement

A compiler-control line of the form

        `#define` *identifier token-string*

(note: no trailing semicolon) causes the preprocessor to replace subsequent instances of the identifier with the given string of tokens. A line of the form

        `#define` *identifier*(*identifier* , ... , *identifier*) *token-string*

where there is no space between the first identifier and the (, is a macro definition with arguments. Subsequent instances of the first identifier followed by a (, a sequence of tokens delimited by commas, and a) are replaced by the token string in the definition. Each occurrence of an identifier mentioned in the formal parameter list of the definition is replaced by the corresponding token string from the call. The actual arguments in the call are token strings separated by commas; however commas in quoted strings or protected by parentheses do not separate arguments. The number of formal and actual parameters must be the same. Text inside a string or a character constant is not subject to replacement.

In both forms the replacement string is rescanned for more defined identifiers. In both forms a long definition may be continued on another line by writing \ at the end of the line to be continued.

This facility is most valuable for definition of "manifest constants," as in

```
#define TABSIZE 100

int table[TABSIZE];
```

A control line of the form

        `#undef` *identifier*

causes the identifier's preprocessor definition to be forgotten.

12.2 File inclusion

A compiler control line of the form

        `#include` *"filename"*

causes the replacement of that line by the entire contents of the file *filename*. The named file is searched for first in the directory of the original source file, and then in a sequence of standard places. Alternatively, a control line of the form

        `#include` *<filename>*

searches only the standard places, and not the directory of the source file.

`#include`'s may be nested.

12.3 Conditional compilation

A compiler control line of the form

> `#if` *constant-expression*

checks whether the constant expression (see §15) evaluates to non-zero. A control line of the form

> `#ifdef` *identifier*

checks whether the identifier is currently defined in the preprocessor; that is, whether it has been the subject of a `#define` control line. A control line of the form

> `#ifndef` *identifier*

checks whether the identifier is currently undefined in the preprocessor.

All three forms are followed by an arbitrary number of lines, possibly containing a control line

> `#else`

and then by a control line

> `#endif`

If the checked condition is true then any lines between `#else` and `#endif` are ignored. If the checked condition is false then any lines between the test and an `#else` or, lacking an `#else`, the `#endif`, are ignored.

These constructions may be nested.

12.4 Line control

For the benefit of other preprocessors which generate C programs, a line of the form

> `#line` *constant identifier*

causes the compiler to believe, for purposes of error diagnostics, that the line number of the next source line is given by the constant and the current input file is named by the identifier. If the identifier is absent the remembered file name does not change.

13. Implicit declarations

It is not always necessary to specify both the storage class and the type of identifiers in a declaration. The storage class is supplied by the context in external definitions and in declarations of formal parameters and structure members. In a declaration inside a function, if a storage class but no type is given, the identifier is assumed to be `int`; if a type but no storage class is indicated, the identifier is assumed to be `auto`. An exception to the latter rule is made for functions, since `auto` functions are meaningless (C being incapable of compiling code into the stack); if the type of an identifier is "function returning ...", it is implicitly declared to be `extern`.

In an expression, an identifier followed by (and not already declared is contextually declared to be "function returning `int`".

14. Types revisited

This section summarizes the operations which can be performed on objects of certain types.

14.1 Structures and unions

There are only two things that can be done with a structure or union: name one of its members (by means of the **.** operator); or take its address (by unary &). Other operations, such as assigning from or to it or passing it as a parameter, draw an error message. In the future, it is expected that these operations, but not necessarily others, will be allowed.

§7.1 says that in a direct or indirect structure reference (with **.** or ->) the name on the right must be a member of the structure named or pointed to by the expression on the left. To allow an escape from the typing rules, this restriction is not firmly enforced by the compiler. In fact, any lvalue is allowed before ., and that lvalue is then assumed to have the form of the structure of which the name on the right is a member. Also, the expression before a -> is required only to be a pointer or an integer. If a pointer, it is assumed to point to a structure of which the name on the right is a member. If an integer, it is taken to be the absolute address, in machine storage units, of the appropriate structure.

Such constructions are non-portable.

14.2 Functions

There are only two things that can be done with a function: call it, or take its address. If the name of a function appears in an expression not in the function-name position of a call, a pointer to the function is generated. Thus, to pass one function to another, one might say

```
int f();
...
g(f);
```

Then the definition of g might read

```
g(funcp)
int (*funcp)();
{
        ...
        (*funcp)();
        ...
}
```

Notice that f must be declared explicitly in the calling routine since its appearance in g(f) was not followed by (.

14.3 Arrays, pointers, and subscripting

Every time an identifier of array type appears in an expression, it is converted into a pointer to the first member of the array. Because of this conversion, arrays are not lvalues. By definition, the subscript operator [] is interpreted in such a way that E1[E2] is identical to *((E1)+(E2)). Because of the conversion rules which apply to +, if E1 is an array and E2 an integer, then E1[E2] refers to the E2-th member of E1. Therefore, despite its asymmetric appearance, subscripting is a commutative operation.

A consistent rule is followed in the case of multi-dimensional arrays. If E is an n-dimensional array of rank $i \times j \times \cdots \times k$, then E appearing in an expression is converted to a pointer to an $(n-1)$-dimensional array with rank $j \times \cdots \times k$. If the * operator, either explicitly or implicitly as a result of subscripting, is applied to this pointer, the result is the pointed-to $(n-1)$-dimensional array, which itself is immediately converted into a pointer.

For example, consider

```
int x[3][5];
```

Here x is a 3×5 array of integers. When x appears in an expression, it is converted to a pointer to (the first of three) 5-membered arrays of integers. In the expression x[i], which is equivalent to *(x+i), x is first converted to a pointer as described; then i is converted to the type of x, which involves multiplying i by the length the object to which the pointer points, namely 5 integer objects. The results are added and indirection applied to yield an array (of 5 integers) which in turn is converted to a pointer to the first of the integers. If there is another subscript the same argument applies again; this time the result is an integer.

It follows from all this that arrays in C are stored row-wise (last subscript varies fastest) and that the first subscript in the declaration helps determine the amount of storage consumed by an array but plays no other part in subscript calculations.

14.4 Explicit pointer conversions

Certain conversions involving pointers are permitted but have implementation-dependent aspects. They are all specified by means of an explicit type-conversion operator, §§7.2 and 8.7.

A pointer may be converted to any of the integral types large enough to hold it. Whether an int or long is required is machine dependent. The mapping function is also machine dependent, but is intended to be unsurprising to those who know the addressing structure of the machine. Details for some particular machines are given below.

An object of integral type may be explicitly converted to a pointer. The mapping always carries an integer converted from a pointer back to the same pointer, but is otherwise machine dependent.

A pointer to one type may be converted to a pointer to another type. The resulting pointer may cause addressing exceptions upon use if the subject pointer does not refer to an object suitably aligned in storage. It is guaranteed that a pointer to an object of a given size may be converted to a pointer to an object of a smaller size and back again without change.

For example, a storage-allocation routine might accept a size (in bytes) of an object to allocate, and return a char pointer; it might be used in this way.

```
extern char *alloc();
double *dp;

dp = (double *) alloc(sizeof(double));
*dp = 22.0 / 7.0;
```

alloc must ensure (in a machine-dependent way) that its return value is suitable for conversion to a pointer to double; then the *use* of the function is portable.

The pointer representation on the PDP-11 corresponds to a 16-bit integer and is measured in bytes. chars have no alignment requirements; everything else must have an even address.

On the Honeywell 6000, a pointer corresponds to a 36-bit integer; the word part is in the left 18 bits, and the two bits that select the character in a word just to their right. Thus char pointers are measured in units of 2^{16} bytes; everything else is measured in units of 2^{18} machine words. double quantities and aggregates containing them must lie on an even word address (0 mod 2^{19}).

The IBM 370 and the Interdata 8/32 are similar. On both, addresses are measured in bytes; elementary objects must be aligned on a boundary equal to their length, so pointers to short must be 0 mod 2, to int and float 0 mod 4, and to double 0 mod 8. Aggregates are aligned on the strictest boundary required by any of their constituents.

15. Constant expressions

In several places C requires expressions which evaluate to a constant: after case, as array bounds, and in initializers. In the first two cases, the expression can involve only integer constants, character constants, and sizeof expressions, possibly connected by the binary operators

$$+ \quad - \quad * \quad / \quad \% \quad \& \quad | \quad \hat{} \quad << \quad >> \quad == \quad != \quad < \quad > \quad <= \quad >=$$

or by the unary operators

$$- \quad \tilde{}$$

or by the ternary operator

$$? :$$

Parentheses can be used for grouping, but not for function calls.

More latitude is permitted for initializers; besides constant expressions as discussed above, one can also apply the unary & operator to external or static objects, and to external or static arrays subscripted with a constant expression. The unary & can also be applied implicitly by appearance of unsubscripted arrays and functions. The basic rule is that initializers must evaluate either to a constant or to the address of a previously declared external or static object plus or minus a constant.

16. Portability considerations

Certain parts of C are inherently machine dependent. The following list of potential trouble spots is not meant to be all-inclusive, but to point out the main ones.

Purely hardware issues like word size and the properties of floating point arithmetic and integer division have proven in practice to be not much of a problem. Other facets of the hardware are reflected in differing implementations. Some of these, particularly sign extension (converting a negative character into a negative integer) and the order in which bytes are placed in a word, are a nuisance that must be carefully watched. Most of the others are only minor problems.

The number of `register` variables that can actually be placed in registers varies from machine to machine, as does the set of valid types. Nonetheless, the compilers all do things properly for their own machine; excess or invalid `register` declarations are ignored.

Some difficulties arise only when dubious coding practices are used. It is exceedingly unwise to write programs that depend on any of these properties.

The order of evaluation of function arguments is not specified by the language. It is right to left on the PDP-11, left to right on the others. The order in which side effects take place is also unspecified.

Since character constants are really objects of type `int`, multi-character character constants are permitted. The specific implementation is very machine dependent, however, because the order in which characters are assigned to a word varies from one machine to another.

Fields are assigned to words and characters to integers right-to-left on the PDP-11 and left-to-right on other machines. These differences are invisible to isolated programs which do not indulge in type punning (for example, by converting an `int` pointer to a `char` pointer and inspecting the pointed-to storage), but must be accounted for when conforming to externally-imposed storage layouts.

The language accepted by the various compilers differs in minor details. Most notably, the current PDP-11 compiler will not initialize structures containing bit-fields, and does not accept a few assignment operators in certain contexts where the value of the assignment is used.

17. Anachronisms

Since C is an evolving language, certain obsolete constructions may be found in older programs. Although most versions of the compiler support such anachronisms, ultimately they will disappear, leaving only a portability problem behind.

Earlier versions of C used the form $=op$ instead of $op=$ for assignment operators. This leads to ambiguities, typified by

```
x=-1
```

which actually decrements `x` since the = and the – are adjacent, but which might easily be intended to assign –1 to `x`.

The syntax of initializers has changed: previously, the equals sign that introduces an initializer was not present, so instead of

```
int  x    = 1;
```

one used

```
int  x    1;
```

The change was made because the initialization

```
int   f      (1+2)
```

resembles a function declaration closely enough to confuse the compilers.

18. Syntax Summary

This summary of C syntax is intended more for aiding comprehension than as an exact statement of the language.

18.1 Expressions

The basic expressions are:

> *expression:*
> > *primary*
> > ∗ *expression*
> > & *expression*
> > − *expression*
> > ! *expression*
> > ˜ *expression*
> > ++ *lvalue*
> > −− *lvalue*
> > *lvalue* ++
> > *lvalue* −−
> > **sizeof** *expression*
> > (*type-name*) *expression*
> > *expression binop expression*
> > *expression* ? *expression* : *expression*
> > *lvalue asgnop expression*
> > *expression* , *expression*

> *primary:*
> > *identifier*
> > *constant*
> > *string*
> > (*expression*)
> > *primary* (*expression-list$_{opt}$*)
> > *primary* [*expression*]
> > *lvalue* . *identifier*
> > *primary* −> *identifier*

> *lvalue:*
> > *identifier*
> > *primary* [*expression*]
> > *lvalue* . *identifier*
> > *primary* −> *identifier*
> > ∗ *expression*
> > (*lvalue*)

The primary-expression operators

> ()   []   .   ->

have highest priority and group left-to-right. The unary operators

```
*   &   -   !   ~   ++   --   sizeof   ( type-name )
```

have priority below the primary operators but higher than any binary operator, and group right-to-left. Binary operators and the conditional operator all group left-to-right, and have priority decreasing as indicated:

binop:
```
*    /    %
+    -
>>   <<
<    >    <=    >=
==   !=
&
^
|
&&
||
?:
```

Assignment operators all have the same priority, and all group right-to-left.

asgnop:
```
=   +=   -=   *=   /=   %=   >>=   <<=   &=   ^=   |=
```

The comma operator has the lowest priority, and groups left-to-right.

18.2 Declarations

declaration:
> *decl-specifiers init-declarator-list*$_{opt}$ **;**

decl-specifiers:
> *type-specifier decl-specifiers*$_{opt}$
> *sc-specifier decl-specifiers*$_{opt}$

sc-specifier:
```
auto
static
extern
register
typedef
```

type-specifier:
>   char
>   short
>   int
>   long
>   unsigned
>   float
>   double
>   *struct-or-union-specifier*
>   *typedef-name*

init-declarator-list:
>   *init-declarator*
>   *init-declarator , init-declarator-list*

init-declarator:
>   *declarator initializer*_{opt}

declarator:
>   *identifier*
>   (*declarator*)
>   * *declarator*
>   *declarator* ( )
>   *declarator* [*constant-expression*_{opt}]

struct-or-union-specifier:
>   struct { *struct-decl-list* }
>   struct *identifier* { *struct-decl-list* }
>   struct *identifier*
>   union { *struct-decl-list* }
>   union *identifier* { *struct-decl-list* }
>   union *identifier*

struct-decl-list:
>   *struct-declaration*
>   *struct-declaration struct-decl-list*

struct-declaration:
>   *type-specifier struct-declarator-list* ;

struct-declarator-list:
>   *struct-declarator*
>   *struct-declarator , struct-declarator-list*

struct-declarator:
    declarator
    declarator **:** *constant-expression*
    : *constant-expression*

initializer:
    = *expression*
    = { *initializer-list* }
    = { *initializer-list* **,** }

initializer-list:
    expression
    initializer-list **,** *initializer-list*
    { *initializer-list* }

type-name:
    type-specifier abstract-declarator

abstract-declarator:
    empty
    (*abstract-declarator*)
    * *abstract-declarator*
    abstract-declarator ( )
    abstract-declarator [*constant-expression*$_{opt}$]

typedef-name:
    identifier

18.3 Statements

compound-statement:
    { *declaration-list*$_{opt}$ *statement-list*$_{opt}$ }

declaration-list:
    declaration
    declaration declaration-list

statement-list:
    statement
    statement statement-list

statement:
        compound-statement
        expression ;
        `if` (*expression*) *statement*
        `if` (*expression*) *statement* `else` *statement*
        `while` (*expression*) *statement*
        `do` *statement* `while` (*expression*) ;
        `for` (*expression-1*$_{opt}$; *expression-2*$_{opt}$; *expression-3*$_{opt}$) *statement*
        `switch` (*expression*) *statement*
        `case` *constant-expression* :   *statement*
        `default` : *statement*
        `break` ;
        `continue` ;
        `return` ;
        `return` *expression* ;
        `goto` *identifier* ;
        identifier : *statement*
        ;

18.4 External definitions

program:
        external-definition
        external-definition program

external-definition:
        function-definition
        data-definition

function-definition:
        type-specifier$_{opt}$ *function-declarator function-body*

function-declarator:
        declarator (*parameter-list*$_{opt}$)

parameter-list:
        identifier
        identifier , *parameter-list*

function-body:
        type-decl-list function-statement

function-statement:
        { *declaration-list*$_{opt}$ *statement-list* }

data-definition:
> **extern**_{opt} *type-specifier*_{opt} *init-declarator-list*_{opt} **;**
> **static**_{opt} *type-specifier*_{opt} *init-declarator-list*_{opt} **;**

18.5 Preprocessor

```
#define identifier token-string
#define identifier( identifier , ... , identifier ) token-string
#undef identifier
#include "filename"
#include <filename>
#if constant-expression
#ifdef identifier
#ifndef identifier
#else
#endif
#line constant identifier
```

INDEX

TEAR OUT THIS PAGE TO ORDER THESE OTHER HIGH QUALITY C LANGUAGE AND UNIX* SYSTEM TITLES FROM THE WORLD'S PREMIER C/UNIX PUBLISHER— PRENTICE-HALL

Quantity	Title/Author	ISBN	Price	Total $
_____	1. The C Programming Language; Kernighan/Ritchie	013–110163–3	$24.95 paper	_____
_____	2. The C Answer Book; Tondo/ Gimpel	013–109877–2	$17.95 paper	_____
_____	3. The UNIX* Programming Environment; Kernighan/Pike	013–937699–2	$26.95 cloth	_____
_____	4. The C Puzzle Book; Feuer	013–109934–5	$21.95 cloth	_____
_____	5. C: A Reference Manual, 2/E Harbison/Steele	013-109810-1	$28.95 cloth	_____
_____	6. The Design of the UNIX* Operating System; Bach	013–201799–7	$31.95 cloth	_____
_____	7. Advanced UNIX* Programming; Rochkind	013–011818–4	$32.95 cloth	_____
_____	8. System Software Tools; Biggerstaff	013–881772–3	$28.95 cloth	_____
_____	9. Crafting C Tools for the IBM PC; Campbell	013–188418–2	$21.95 paper	_____
_____	10. The UNIX* System User's Handbook; AT&T	013–937764–6	$16.95 paper	_____
_____	11. The Vi User's Handbook; AT&T	013–941733–8	$16.95 paper	_____
_____	12. The C Programmer's Handbook; AT&T	013–110073–4	$16.95 paper	_____
_____	13. AT&T Computer Software Catalog: MS DOS; AT&T	0–8359–9278–0	$19.95 paper	_____
_____	14. AT&T Computer Software Catalog: UNIX* System V; AT&T	0–8359–9279–0	$19.95 paper	_____
_____	15. The UNIX* C Shell Field Guide; Anderson/Anderson	013–937468–X	$23.95 paper	_____
_____	16. DOS/UNIX*: Becoming A Super User; Seyer/Mills	013–218645–4	$21.95 paper	_____
_____	17. UNIX* RefGuide; McNulty Development, Inc.	013–938952–0	$24.95 paper	_____
_____	18. Preparing Documents With UNIX*; Brown	013–699976–X	$21.95 cloth	_____
_____	19. Learning to Program in C; Plum	013–527854–6	$34.95 cloth	_____
_____	20. Programming in C With a Bit of UNIX*; Moore	013–730094–8	$22.95 paper	_____

			Total $	_____
			– discount (if appropriate)	_____
			New Total $	_____

OVER PLEASE

AND TAKE ADVANTAGE OF THESE SPECIAL OFFERS!

a.) When ordering 3 or 4 copies (of the same or different titles), take 10% off the total list price (excluding sales tax, where applicable).

b.) When ordering 5 to 20 copies (of the same or different titles), take 15% off the total list price (excluding sales tax, where applicable).

c.) To receive a greater discount when ordering 20 or more copies, call or write:

Special Sales Department
College Marketing
Prentice-Hall
Englewood Cliffs, NJ 07632
201-592-2498

SAVE!
If payment accompanies order, plus your state's sales tax where applicable, Prentice-Hall pays postage and handling charges. Same return privilege refund guaranteed. Please do not mail in cash.

☐ **PAYMENT ENCLOSED**—shipping and handling to be paid by publisher (please include your state's tax where applicable).

☐ **SEND BOOKS ON 15-DAY TRIAL BASIS** & bill me (with small charge for shipping and handling).

Name_____

Address_____

City_____ State_____ Zip_____

I prefer to charge my ☐Visa ☐MasterCard

Card Number_____ Expiration Date_____

Signature_____
All prices listed are subject to change without notice.

Mail your order to: Prentice-Hall, Book Distribution Center, Route 59 at
Brook Hill Drive, West Nyack, NY 10994

Dept. 1   D–TMAR–LR(7)